COUNTDOWN TO COMMON CORE ASSESSMENTS

English Language Arts

Mc
Graw
Hill
Education

Bothell, WA • Chicago, IL • Columbus, OH • New York, NY

www.mheonline.com

Send all inquiries to:
McGraw-Hill Education
Two Penn Plaza
New York, New York 10121

ISBN: 978-0-02-135109-1
MHID: 0-02-135109-0

Printed in the United States of America.

1 2 3 4 5 6 7 8 9 RHR 18 17 16 15 14 13

A

Table of Contents

Countdown to Common Core Assessments: English Language Arts

Countdown to Common Core Assessments: English Language Arts is an integral part of a complete assessment program aligned to the Common Core State Standards (CCSS). The advances in assessment featured in the Performance-Based Tasks and End-of-Year Assessment include passages and stimulus texts that reflect the increased text complexity and rigor required by the CCSS. The test items require higher-order thinking skills, emphasize the need for students to support responses with text evidence, and feature writing as the result of research, with prompts requiring student understanding of and engagement with the stimulus texts. In a departure from previous high-stakes assessments, individual items align to multiple standards.

NOTE: These tests are intended to familiarize students with the types of items they may encounter on the Common Core assessments. The test scores will provide you with a general idea of how well students have mastered the various skills; the scores are *not* intended to be used for classroom grading purposes.

Overview of Performance-Based Tasks

The Performance-Based Tasks provide students with scenarios that establish a unified purpose for reading and writing. Two distinct types of performance-based tasks are provided. The first five tasks are similar to the tasks students are likely to encounter in states that participate in the Partnership for Assessment of Readiness for College and Careers (PARCC) consortium. The second five tasks are similar to the tasks students are likely to encounter in states that participate in the Smarter Balanced Assessment Consortium.

All of the performance-based tasks provided in this book are appropriate for use in any state, whether consortia-affiliated or independent. Use these tasks in any combination to increase students' comfort level with and understanding of the range of CCSS assessments they may encounter.

Task and Item Types

All of the performance-based tasks assess student integration of knowledge and skills. Each task assesses multiple standards that address comprehension, research skills, genre writing, and the use of English language conventions. The stimulus texts and questions in each task build toward the goal of the final writing topic. Students write across texts to demonstrate their understanding of key elements underpinning the multiple sources.

Each PARCC-style assessment comprises three distinct tasks—**Narrative Writing, Literary Analysis,** and **Research Simulation.** Selected response items generally have two distinct parts. In Part A, students answer a text-based question; in Part B, they support their answer with evidence from the text. The Narrative Writing task uses a single stimulus passage; the Prose Constructed Response (PCR) asks students to complete or further develop the passage in a manner consistent with the existing story elements. PCR items in the Literary Analysis and Research Simulation tasks ask students to craft written essays in response to a variety of stimulus texts.

Each Smarter Balanced-style assessment consists of one of three distinct tasks—**Narrative, Opinion,** or **Informational.** The tasks employ a range of item types to measure student understanding. Research Questions include both selected-response and constructed-response items that test students' comprehension of the stimulus texts and help them to synthesize the information provided by the texts. Students then are directed to craft a written response to the texts and questions.

Administering and Scoring the Performance-Based Tasks

Administer each performance-based task separately. For planning purposes, use the suggested times given below.

- Allow 50 minutes for the Narrative Writing task, 80 minutes for the Literary Analysis task, and 80 minutes for the Research Simulation task.
- Allow 105 minutes for completion of each Narrative, Opinion, and Informational task. During the first 35 minutes, students will read the stimulus materials and answer the research questions; after a short break, students will use the remaining 70 minutes for planning, writing, and editing their responses.

Scoring the Selected-Response and Research Questions

Each Narrative Writing, Literary Analysis, and Research Simulation selected-response item is worth 2 points.

Score two-part items as follows:

- 2 points if both Part A and Part B are correct
- 1 point if Part A is correct and Part B is incorrect or partially correct
- 0 points if Part A is incorrect, even if Part B is correct

Score one-part items as follows:

- 2 points if correct
- 1 point if partially correct
- 0 points if incorrect

For the Narrative, Opinion, and Informational task Research Questions, selected-response items are worth 1 point and constructed-response items are worth 2 points.

Scoring the Essays

Score the Narrative Writing, Literary Analysis, and Research Simulation PCRs holistically on a 16-point scale. Point values are broken down as follows:

- 3 points for addressing the relevant reading comprehension standards [R]
- 9 points for addressing the relevant writing standards [W]
- 4 points for addressing the relevant language conventions standards [L]

A PCR scoring rubric follows the Answer Keys to help you score the essays.

Score the Narrative, Opinion, and Informational task essays holistically on a 10-point scale. Point values are broken down as follows:

- 4 points for purpose/organization [P/O]
- 4 points for evidence/elaboration [E/E] or development/elaboration [D/E]
- 2 points for English language conventions [C]

Genre-specific scoring rubrics follow the Answer Keys to help you score the essays.

Answer Keys

In addition to the responses to the test items, the Answer Keys identify CCSS correlations. The Narrative, Opinion, and Informational task Answer Keys also identify claims and targets met, Depth of Knowledge (DOK), and level of difficulty. You can copy the Answer Keys and use them to track each student's scores.

Overview of End-of-Year Assessment

The End-of-Year Assessment focuses on reading and vocabulary skills, which are assessed by selected-response items. RI or RL standard 1 is the structural component underlying every comprehension item. Additional grade-level comprehension and vocabulary standards address the identification and use of supporting text evidence.

Administering and Scoring the End-of-Year Assessment

Administer the End-of-Year Assessment in two or three sessions, with a short break between each session. For planning purposes, allow 140 minutes per test, excluding the break periods.

Each of the 26 items is worth 2 points. The Answer Key provides a scoring column to create a 52-point test, with multi-part questions eligible for partial credit. In addition to the responses to the test items, the Answer Key identifies CCSS correlations. You can copy the Answer Key and use it to track each student's scores.

Score two-part items as follows:

- 2 points if both Part A and Part B are correct
- 1 point if Part A is correct and Part B is incorrect or partially correct
- 0 points if Part A is incorrect, even if Part B is correct

Score one-part items as follows:

- 2 points if correct
- 1 point if partially correct
- 0 points if incorrect

NOTE: If you prefer to give all items equal weight, give full credit only for completely correct answers and no credit for partially correct answers.

Narrative Writing 1

Today you will read a story titled "The Rebirth of Happiness." As you read, pay close attention to the plot of the story. You will then answer questions to prepare to write a narrative story.

Read the story "The Rebirth of Happiness" and answer the questions that follow.

The Rebirth of Happiness

1   Nothing burns like the cold, penetrating winds and heavy snowstorms of winter. They are a cruel joke from Mother Nature. Darkness comes early, leaving little time to enjoy the sun, and in many regions, winter is harsh, numbing, and bitter.

2   The first day at my new school was as rude as a rugged winter. I was forced to adjust to a new environment, but my surroundings didn't seem to adjust to me. It was just two weeks shy of spring, and I felt like a fish out of water. Students, teachers, and that maze of a school building were too foreign for comfort.

3   "Excuse me, but is this Room 106?"

4   I didn't get a response, only stares, not even when I tripped over a chair as I walked to my desk, although I suppose I should have felt grateful that no one laughed. Was this what I had to look forward to all year?

5   "Don't worry," said Mom, "I know that starting a new school can be tough, but look at the bright side of things. Spring is coming, and that's your favorite time of year."

6   Mom always had soothing words to lift my spirits. She was right, too, and the wheels of change had begun to turn. The birds were back and chirping louder than ever. The grass was greener and the flowers were beginning to bloom, like a breath of fresh air!

7   One day shortly after, I heard the phone ringing from down the hall, and Mom suddenly appeared in the doorway.

8   "Desiree, the phone is for you. It's one of your classmates . . . ."

GO ON →

1 **Part A:** What is the meaning of the word **penetrating** as it is used in paragraph 1?

(A) mysterious

(B) invisible

(C) pleasant

(D) strong

Part B: Which excerpt from paragraph 1 helps the reader understand the meaning of **penetrating**?

(A) "Nothing burns like the cold . . ."

(B) ". . . snowstorms of winter."

(C) "Darkness comes early . . ."

(D) ". . . little time to enjoy . . ."

2 **Part A:** How does the setting change from the beginning of the story to the end of the story?

(A) Desiree goes to a different school.

(B) The weather gets warmer.

(C) Desiree moves to a new home.

(D) The students begin to act nicer.

Part B: Which detail shows the importance of the setting in the story?

(A) Desiree's mom gives her good advice.

(B) Desiree does not make new friends quickly.

(C) Desiree hears the phone ring down the hall.

(D) Desiree's favorite season of the year is spring.

GO ON →

3 Select **one** phrase that shows how Desiree feels in winter and **one** phrase that shows how she feels in spring. Write the phrases in the chart.

Phrases:

two weeks shy of spring   tripped over a chair

like a breath of fresh air   too foreign for comfort

first day at my new school   heard the phone ringing

Desiree's Point of View in Winter	Desiree's Point of View in Spring
_____ _____	_____ _____

GO ON →

4 **Part A:** Which sentence describes how the story is organized?

Ⓐ It is divided into two parts based on the time of year.

Ⓑ It is divided into two parts based on Desiree and her mom's point of view.

Ⓒ It is divided into three parts based on the different schools that Desiree attends.

Ⓓ It is divided into three parts based on the different experiences Desiree has at school.

Part B: Underline **two** details about the story that help to explain how it is organized.

Ⓐ Desiree's classroom is Room 106.

Ⓑ Desiree's classroom is filled with students.

Ⓒ Desiree's first day of school is at the end of winter.

Ⓓ Desiree's mom is good at cheering up Desiree.

Ⓔ Desiree begins to feel better when the birds come back.

Ⓕ Desiree's mom answers the phone and speaks to a classmate.

GO ON →

5 **Part A:** Which statement expresses the theme of the story?

   Ⓐ Better to arrive late than never.

   Ⓑ True friends are hard to come by.

   Ⓒ Do not try to be someone you are not.

   Ⓓ Tomorrow brings hope for new beginnings.

Part B: Which detail from the story is an example of this theme?

   Ⓐ The birds chirp loudly.

   Ⓑ The phone rings.

   Ⓒ Desiree dislikes the cold.

   Ⓓ Desiree goes to a new school.

GO ON →

6 In the story, Desiree struggles to get used to going to a new school. Think about how her point of view changes. The story ends when the phone rings, and Desiree finds out that a classmate is calling her.

Write an original story to continue where this one ended. In your story, be sure to use what you know about Desiree and her experiences to tell what happens next.

Use the space below to plan your writing. Write your story on a separate sheet of paper.

Narrative Writing 2

Today you will read an article titled "How to Enjoy Dim Sum." As you read the text, you will gather information and answer questions about eating a dim sum meal so you can write a narrative description.

Read the article "How to Enjoy Dim Sum" and answer the questions that follow.

How to Enjoy Dim Sum

1   The next time your family is looking for a special meal, consider dim sum. Dim sum is a traditional Chinese meal. At a dim sum restaurant, servers walk from table to table with rolling carts filled with small, appetizer-like dishes of food. Customers point to what they want and receive the food immediately. The next time the cart comes by, customers can order more food.

2   Dim sum can be confusing and even overwhelming for beginners. Follow these tips to get the most out of your dim sum experience.

3   **Tip 1: Know before you go.** Do some research on typical dim sum foods. Some restaurants provide written menus of what the carts are carrying, but many do not. With some preparation, you can avoid getting overwhelmed by all the choices. Some of the most popular dishes are siu mai (meat dumplings), cha siu bao (steamed pork buns), and har gow (shrimp dumplings). Always remember that your servers can help—so if you want to know what's inside that fried dumpling, just ask!

4   **Tip 2: Be adventurous.** One of the best things about dim sum is the variety. You don't have to commit to eating just one dish, as you do in most restaurants, so this is your opportunity to try small amounts of many different foods.

5   **Tip 3: Pace yourself.** If you don't get what you want the first time around, don't worry. You'll get additional chances when the cart rolls by again. If you take too much right away, you'll get full, and the meal will become expensive.

GO ON →

1 **Part A:** What is the meaning of the word **variety** as it is used in paragraph 4?

(A) wide range of choices

(B) speed of service

(C) number of restaurants

(D) international eating style

Part B: Select **two** phrases from the article that help the reader understand the meaning of **variety**.

(A) "... tips to get the most out of your dim sum experience ..." (Paragraph 2)

(B) "... remember that your servers can help ..." (Paragraph 3)

(C) "... don't have to commit to eating just one ..." (Paragraph 4)

(D) "... as you do in most restaurants ..." (Paragraph 4)

(E) "... small amounts of many different foods." (Paragraph 4)

(F) "... additional chances when the cart rolls by again." (Paragraph 5)

GO ON →

2 **Part A:** What is the **best** way for a researcher reading this article to locate quick information about how dim sum customers should pace their eating?

(A) review the title

(B) look at the captions

(C) scan the boldface headings

(D) read the article out loud

Part B: Which part of the article supports the answer to Part A?

(A) "... receive the food immediately." (Paragraph 1)

(B) "Follow these tips to get the most ..." (Paragraph 2)

(C) "**Tip 1: Know before you go.**" (Paragraph 3)

(D) "**Tip 3: Pace yourself.**" (Paragraph 5)

GO ON →

3 **Part A:** What reason does the author provide to support the point that dim sum beginners could use some tips?

(A) Doing research on typical foods cannot prepare beginners.

(B) Most customers do not know how to be adventurous.

(C) The servers at dim sum restaurants are helpful to customers.

(D) The unique eating style can make decisions difficult.

Part B: Which sentence from the article **best** illustrates the answer to Part A?

(A) "The next time your family is looking for a special meal, consider dim sum." (Paragraph 1)

(B) "Customers point to what they want and receive the food immediately." (Paragraph 1)

(C) "With some preparation, you can avoid getting overwhelmed by all the choices." (Paragraph 3)

(D) "If you take too much right away, you'll get full, and the meal will become expensive." (Paragraph 5)

GO ON →

4   **Part A:** Which detail is the most important to include in a summary of the article?

(A) Customers have multiple opportunities to order food.

(B) Cha siu bao is Chinese for "steamed pork buns."

(C) Servers are available to answer questions about dishes.

(D) If you order a lot of food, the meal can get pricey.

Part B: Which sentence from the article **best** reveals the detail in Part A?

(A) "Dim sum can be confusing and even overwhelming for beginners." (Paragraph 2)

(B) "Some of the most popular dishes are siu mai (meat dumplings), cha siu bao (steamed pork buns), and har gow (shrimp dumplings)." (Paragraph 3)

(C) "One of the best things about dim sum is the variety." (Paragraph 4)

(D) "You'll get additional chances when the cart rolls by again." (Paragraph 5)

GO ON →

5 The following main ideas are contained in the article: dim sum restaurants are different from other restaurants, and dim sum dishes do not contain large amounts of food. Underline **one** sentence in paragraph 1 that includes details supporting both main ideas.

> The next time your family is looking for a special meal, consider dim sum. Dim sum is a traditional Chinese meal. At a dim sum restaurant, servers walk from table to table with rolling carts filled with small, appetizer-like dishes of food. Customers point to what they want and receive the food immediately. The next time the cart comes by, customers can order more food.

GO ON →

6 A class is researching the topic, "Appreciating different cultures." The goal is to study ways to experience the traditions of a variety of cultures. You are assigned to narrate and describe an experience at a dim sum restaurant.

Using the article "How to Enjoy Dim Sum," write a narrative that shares what it is like to order and eat dim sum in a restaurant. To create a well-written narrative:

- Use relevant details from the article to support your description of going out for dim sum. The details may be stated in the article or inferred from the text. Any inferences you draw should be based on text evidence.

- Organize the narrative to make important connections between the characteristics of a typical dim sum meal and the descriptive details you include.

- Use narrative techniques where appropriate, such as point of view and pacing, to make sure readers understand the cultural characteristics of dim sum.

Use the space below to plan your writing. Write the narrative on a separate sheet of paper.

Literary Analysis 1

Today you will read a story titled "The Great Debate." You will also read a poem titled "The Juvenile Orator." As you read, consider how the narrator's point of view in the story is similar to the speaker's point of view in the poem. You will be asked to write a comparison of the narrator and the speaker's points of view.

Read the story "The Great Debate" and answer the questions that follow.

The Great Debate

1   The lights were dim and the curtains closed. There were several mini conversations among the hundred or so students in the audience, but the butterflies in my stomach overpowered the noise. I glanced over at my opponent, and she didn't appear to have a care in the world. That made me even more nervous.

2   "Good afternoon, students of McGavin K-8 School."

3   A hush came over the crowd for Mr. Henderson, our principal. His presence was commanding. When he spoke, no one dared to utter a word.

4   "We are here today to witness school history. For the first time, there will be a fifth-grader running for Student Body President."

5   "Hooray, Hoorah!" There was a brief but loud bolt of cheers from a group of fifth-graders seated in the back of the auditorium.

6   "Today, Mario Gomez will face off against our current student body president and seventh-grader, Celia Boone. The moderator will present one question to each candidate, who has five minutes to respond to the question. I ask that all students hold their applause until the end of the five-minute response time."

7   Neither Celia nor I knew who would be addressed first or what question was going to be asked. We both knew, however, that our response could mean victory or defeat. I had a lot riding on this debate. I had big plans to change how our school was run, but was I too young to make a significant difference?

8   The moderator grasped the microphone. "Good afternoon, candidates. The first question is for Celia. Explain one major change last year that you encouraged the McGavin faculty to make—one that you are particularly proud of."

9   As Celia began answering the question, I practically could have finished her response for her. She's always seemed to have a "cookie-cutter response" for everything. I knew that Celia was going to give the audience a five-minute explanation of how she had encouraged the staff to repurchase the vending machines that they'd gotten rid of just two years prior.

GO ON →

10   "I'm most proud of getting the vending machines, something that we all love, placed back into the hallways of McGavin—something my opponent is too young to even know about—"

11   As she responded to the question, I remained lost in my own thoughts. I was too worried about my question to be concerned about Celia taking jabs at my age.

12   "Thank you, Celia." The audience's applause let me know that Celia's five minutes had come and gone.

13   "Mario Gomez, will your age affect your ability to stimulate change?"

14   I was ready for this type of question, and I dove right in with my response.

15   "Quality leadership has little to do with someone's age, but more to do with their willingness to take action. I am fully aware of the concerns of the student body and for the past two years, I have been a student council representative, surveying students in all grades on what they think is important—even the vending machines. There have been many young pioneers who were doubted because of their age. Imagine if someone had told Alexander the Great that his age would prevent him from becoming a great warrior and leader. I am wise beyond my years—wise enough to know that there are issues greater than vending machines. Vote for me, not because of my age, but because I *will* stimulate change."

16   When I finished, there was an overwhelming response from the crowd, which included a standing ovation. I gave a huge sigh of relief. I was thrilled to know that the students at McGavin wanted change as much as I did.

GO ON →

1 **Part A:** What does the word **utter** mean as it is used in paragraph 3?

(A) think about

(B) hold back

(C) write down

(D) say aloud

Part B: Which phrase from paragraph 3 helps the reader understand the meaning of **utter**?

(A) "... hush came over ..."

(B) "... our principal ..."

(C) "... his presence ..."

(D) "... was commanding ..."

GO ON →

2 **Part A:** What is a theme of the story?

(A) Let your heart tell you what to do.

(B) What some find easy, others find hard.

(C) Appearances can be deceiving.

(D) Do not be afraid to say what you feel.

Part B: Which sentence from the story supports the theme?

(A) "We both knew, however, that our response could mean victory or defeat." (Paragraph 7)

(B) "As Celia began answering the question, I practically could have finished her response for her." (Paragraph 9)

(C) "The audience's applause let me know that Celia's five minutes had come and gone." (Paragraph 12)

(D) "There have been many young pioneers who were doubted because of their age." (Paragraph 15)

GO ON →

3 **Part A:** How is the narrator different from his opponent, Celia Boone?

(A) He is more experienced at public speaking.

(B) He is interested in improving the school.

(C) He is not knowledgeable about the school.

(D) He is less confident in his ability to help.

Part B: Underline **two** sentences in paragraphs 15 and 16 below that help to explain how the narrator is different from his opponent.

"Quality leadership has little to do with someone's age, but more to do with their willingness to take action. I am fully aware of the concerns of the student body and for the past two years, I have been a student council representative, surveying students in all grades on what they think is important—even the vending machines. There have been many young pioneers who were doubted because of their age. Imagine if someone had told Alexander the Great that his age would prevent him from becoming a great warrior and leader. I am wise beyond my years—wise enough to know that there are issues greater than vending machines. Vote for me, not because of my age, but because I *will* stimulate change."

When I finished, there was an overwhelming response from the crowd, which included a standing ovation. I gave a huge sigh of relief. I was thrilled to know that the students at McGavin wanted change as much as I did.

GO ON →

Read the poem "The Juvenile Orator" and answer the questions that follow.

adapted from
The Juvenile Orator

by David Everett

	You'd not expect one of my age
	To speak in public, on the stage;
	And if I chance to fall below
	Demosthenes or Cicero[1],
5	Don't view me with a critic's eye,
	But pass my many errors by.
	Large streams from little fountains flow;
	Tall oaks from little acorns grow;
	And though I now am small and young,
10	Of judgment weak, and feeble tongue,
	Yet all great famous men—like me—
	Once learned to read their A, B, Cs.
	And why may not this new soil
	Raise men as great as Britain's isle,
15	Above what Greece and Rome have done,
	Or any land beneath the sun?
	May not Massachusetts prove as great
	As any other sister state?
	Or, where's the town, go far or near,

Demosthenes or Cicero[1]—great public speakers from ancient Rome and Greece

GO ON →

Grade 5 • **Performance-Based Tasks**

20 That does not find a rival here?

Or, where is the boy but three feet high

Who's made improvement more than I?

Those thoughts inspire my youthful mind

To be the greatest of mankind;

25 Great, not like **Caesar**[2], stained with blood;

But only great, as I am good.

Caesar[2]—a Roman emperor known for his victories through battles

GO ON →

4 **Part A:** What does the word **rival** mean in line 20 of the poem?

(A) opponent

(B) assistant

(C) supporter

(D) troublemaker

Part B: Which of the following in the poem might represent a **rival** to the speaker?

(A) Cicero

(B) Greece

(C) Rome

(D) Caesar

5 **Part A:** What does the speaker mean in lines 9 through 12 of the poem?

> And though I now am small and young,
> Of judgment weak, and feeble tongue,
> Yet all great famous men—like me—
> Once learned to read their A, B, Cs.

(A) To become a great speaker, one must be smart.

(B) All great speakers had to learn the basics.

(C) To become a great speaker, one must be famous.

(D) All young speakers first learned the alphabet.

Part B: Select **two** other lines in the poem that present the same idea.

(A) To speak in public, on the stage; (Line 2)

(B) Don't view me with a critic's eye, (Line 5)

(C) Large streams from little fountains flow; (Line 7)

(D) Tall oaks from little acorns grow; (Line 8)

(E) Or, where is the boy but three feet high (Line 21)

(F) Those thoughts inspire my youthful mind (Line 23)

GO ON →

6 At line 13 in the poem, the speaker begins to talk about America. Select **three** words that describe the speaker's attitude about this topic. Write them in the box.

Proud
Surprised
Amused
Sure
Excited

<u>**How the Speaker Feels about America**</u>

1. _____

2. _____

3. _____

GO ON →

7 Both the narrator of "The Great Debate" and the speaker of "The Juvenile Orator" have strong viewpoints about speaking in public. Each point of view helps determine how events are described. Write an essay that compares these viewpoints. In your essay, be sure to:

- Use important details from both passages about the viewpoints of the narrator and the speaker. The details may be stated in the passages or inferences you make from the texts. Any inferences you draw should be based on text evidence.

- Organize the essay to compare these viewpoints.

Use the space below to plan your writing. Write your essay on a separate sheet of paper.

Literary Analysis 2

Today you will analyze an excerpt from a Northern European myth titled "The Building of the Wall" and a brief dramatic scene titled "Up Against a Wall." As you read, consider the events of each text. You will be asked to compare and contrast the events at the end of the task.

Read the excerpt from "The Building of the Wall" and answer the questions that follow.

from *The Building of the Wall*
retold by Padraic Colum

1   There are many stories to be told about the gods, but the first one that should be told to you is the one about the building of their City.

2   The gods had made their way up to the top of a high mountain, and there they decided to build a great City for themselves that the Giants could never overthrow. The City they would call "Asgard," which means the Place of the Gods. They would build it on a beautiful plain that was on the top of that high mountain. And they wanted to raise round their City the highest and strongest wall that had ever been built.

3   Now one day when they were beginning to build their halls and their palaces a strange being came to them. Odin, the Father of the Gods, went and spoke to him. "What dost thou want on the Mountain of the Gods?" he asked the Stranger.

4   "I know what is in the mind of the gods," the Stranger said. "They would build a City here. I cannot build palaces, but I can build great walls that can never be overthrown. Let me build the wall round your City."

5   "How long will it take you to build a wall that will go round our City?" said the Father of the Gods.

6   "A year, O Odin," said the Stranger.

7   Now Odin knew that if a great wall could be built around it the gods would not have to spend all their time defending their City, Asgard, from the Giants, and he knew that if Asgard were protected, he himself could go amongst men and teach them and help them. He thought that no payment the Stranger could ask would be too much for the building of that wall.

8   That day the Stranger came to the Council of the Gods, and he swore that in a year he would have the great wall built. Then Odin made an oath that the gods would give him what he asked in payment if the wall was finished to the last stone in a year from that day.

GO ON →

9 | The Stranger went away and came back on the morrow. It was the first day of summer when he started work. He brought no one to help him except a great horse.

10 | Now the gods thought that this horse would do no more than drag blocks of stone for the building of the wall. But the horse did more than this. He set the stones in their places and mortared them together. And day and night and by light and dark the horse worked, and soon a great wall was rising round the palaces that the gods themselves were building.

11 | "What reward will the Stranger ask for the work he is doing for us?" the gods asked one another.

12 | Odin went to the Stranger. "We marvel at the work you and your horse are doing for us," he said. "No one can doubt that the great wall of Asgard will be built up by the first day of summer. What reward do you claim? We would have it ready for you."

13 | The Stranger turned from the work he was doing, leaving the great horse to pile up the blocks of stone. "O Father of the Gods," he said, "O Odin, the reward I shall ask for my work is the Sun and the Moon, and Freya, who watches over the flowers and grasses, for my wife."

1 **Part A:** What is the meaning of the word **overthrow** as it is used in paragraph 2?

(A) reorganize

(B) help build

(C) climb on top of

(D) take control of

Part B: Select **two** phrases from the myth that help the reader understand the meaning of **overthrow**.

(A) ". . . they wanted to raise round their City the highest and strongest wall that had ever been built." (Paragraph 2)

(B) ". . . when they were beginning to build their halls and their palaces a strange being came to them." (Paragraph 3)

(C) ". . . if a great wall could be built around it the gods would not have to spend all their time defending their City, Asgard, from the Giants . . ." (Paragraph 7)

(D) ". . . the gods would give him what he asked in payment if the wall was finished to the last stone in a year . . ." (Paragraph 8)

(E) ". . . this horse would do no more than drag blocks of stone . . ." (Paragraph 10)

(F) "We marvel at the work you and your horse are doing for us . . ." (Paragraph 12)

GO ON →

2 **Part A:** In the myth, the Stranger states his ideas twice—first to Odin and then to the Council of the Gods. How are the events in paragraphs 4 and 8 different?

(A) The second event does not involve Odin.

(B) In the second event, the Stranger changes his ideas.

(C) The second event is formal and more serious.

(D) In the second event, Odin disapproves of the Stranger's ideas.

Part B: Which phrase from paragraph 8 **best** supports the answer to Part A?

(A) ". . . he swore that . . ."

(B) ". . . would have the great wall built . . ."

(C) ". . . give him what he asked . . ."

(D) ". . . the wall was finished . . ."

GO ON →

3 Organize the details from the box in the correct locations on the chart to show how Odin and the Stranger are different. Write all details in the chart for full credit.

Odin		The Stranger	
Character Trait	Text Evidence	Character Trait	Text Evidence

Character Traits:
clever   formal   giving   confident

Text Evidence:
". . . he knew that if Asgard were protected, he himself could go amongst men and teach them and help them."

". . . I can build great walls that can never be overthrown."

"But the horse did more than this. He set the stones in their places and mortared them together."

"What dost thou want on the Mountain of the Gods?"

GO ON →

Read the scene titled "Up Against a Wall" and answer the questions that follow.

Up Against a Wall

SETTING: A school cafeteria. At the center of the room is a team of three fifth-graders: DYLAN, LAUREN, and ALEJANDRO. Their leader, a college student named KEISHA, approaches with a box in her arms.

LAUREN: We're ready for the challenge, Keisha.

KEISHA: Here's the After-School Adventurers Challenge of the Week, which comes directly from Mr. Batra: we've got twenty minutes to build the highest wall, using only the materials that are in this box, starting . . . NOW!

Keisha empties the contents of the box onto the floor.

DYLAN: Paper clips, paper-towel rolls, and rubber bands . . . we're supposed to construct a *wall* with these miscellaneous materials?

ALEJANDRO: I know—let's start a chain that's made of interlocking paper clips and rubber bands.

Alejandro demonstrates, and the others help, but eventually their creation topples to the floor.

DYLAN: To fix this catastrophe, if only we had some glue and twisty ties . . .

LAUREN: Guys, we've got to focus because we've got—how many minutes left, Keisha?

KEISHA: Ten.

LAUREN: Okay, my turn: I think that we should attach the paper clips to the cardboard rolls.

ALEJANDRO: That's a totally different strategy, and you just reminded us that we have to focus!

LAUREN: My plan is focused, because we're going to use only two materials, which I like to call simplification.

DYLAN: I think I understand where you're headed, Lauren. (*Creates a tripod out of paper-towel rolls and paper clips.*)

GO ON →

LAUREN: Absolutely; that's my inspiration!

Using their new strategy, the students build a three-foot-high wall.

KEISHA: Time's up, everyone!

DYLAN: I forgot we were being timed, but I don't really care if we won or not. Let's just keep building!

LAUREN and ALEJANDRO nod enthusiastically.

4 **Part A:** The word **focus** is used in a line spoken by Alejandro.

> "That's a totally different strategy, and you just reminded us that we have to focus!"

What is the meaning of the word **focus** as it is used in the scene?

(A) change the sharpness or quality of a picture

(B) concentrate and bring down to a basic level

(C) think very quickly

(D) ask others for help

Part B: Which phrase from the scene helps the reader understand the meaning of **focus**?

(A) "... we've got twenty minutes to build the highest wall ..."

(B) "... we've got—how many minutes left, Keisha?"

(C) "... going to use only two materials, which I like to call simplification."

(D) "... I understand where you're headed, Lauren."

GO ON →

5 **Part A:** In the scene, the team makes two attempts to build their wall. How are these two events different?

(A) Two different students take the lead in each event.

(B) The students are not being timed during the second round.

(C) The first time, the team has a disagreement with Keisha.

(D) The second time, the team uses a different box of materials.

Part B: Which detail from the scene **best** supports the answer to Part A?

(A) "... we're supposed to construct a *wall* with these ..."

(B) "... *their creation topples to the floor.*"

(C) "... if only we had some glue ..."

(D) "Okay, my turn ..."

GO ON →

6 Underline a detail from the lines below that illustrates the theme that teamwork can be more rewarding than competition.

> **ALEJANDRO:** That's a totally different strategy, and you just reminded us that we have to focus!
>
> **LAUREN:** My plan *is* focused, because we're going to use only two materials, which I like to call simplification.
>
> **DYLAN:** I think I understand where you're headed, Lauren. (*Creates a tripod out of paper-towel rolls and paper clips.*)
>
> **LAUREN:** Absolutely; that's my inspiration!
>
> *Using their new strategy, the students build a three-foot-high wall.*
>
> **KEISHA:** Time's up, everyone!
>
> **DYLAN:** I forgot we were being timed, but I don't really care if we won or not. Let's just keep building!
>
> *LAUREN and ALEJANDRO nod enthusiastically.*

GO ON →

7 "The Building of the Wall" and "Up Against a Wall" have the same main plot event: the construction of a wall. Write an essay that compares and contrasts the two versions of this central event. In your essay, be sure to:

- Consider who builds the wall, as well as how, where, and why it is built.

- Use important details from both passages about the plot lines. The details may be stated in the passages or inferences you make from the texts. Any inferences you draw should be based on text evidence.

- Organize the essay to compare and contrast the two versions of the same event.

Use the space below to plan your writing. Write your essay on a separate sheet of paper.

Research Simulation

Humans have mapped the globe, yet most of our ocean remains unexplored. Many of the sea's fascinating creatures are still a mystery.

Today, you will read an article about the state of ocean exploration and what awaits divers at the bottom of the sea. Then you will read a description of important underwater technology and a brief biography of an ocean explorer and inventor.

As you read these texts, you will gather information and answer questions about deep-sea exploration. At the end of the task, you will be asked to write an essay about the topic.

Read the article "Oceans: Earth's Final Frontier" and answer the questions that follow.

Oceans: Earth's Final Frontier

1   In the past 50 years, explorers have set their sights on the stars. Our ships have orbited Jupiter, Saturn, Venus, and Mercury. However, many scientists believe explorers should now turn their attention *down* instead of up. According to these experts, the oceans are Earth's last unexplored frontier.

2   Seventy percent of our planet lies under water. This "world ocean" consists of the Pacific, our largest ocean, followed by the Atlantic, Indian, Southern, and Arctic Oceans. We have explored less than 5 percent of these waters. In fact, we have better maps of the surface of Mars than we do of our oceans.

Underwater Geography

3   What's so exciting about exploring the bottom of the ocean? Actually, the ocean bottom contains as many different features as our continents.

- **Mountains** The longest mountain range in the world is completely under water. Called the Mid-Atlantic Ridge, it stretches for more than 35,000 miles. This chain of mountains runs across the Atlantic Ocean and into parts of the Indian and Pacific Oceans.

- **Valleys** The ocean also contains deep valleys. The deepest place on Earth— the Mariana Trench—plunges seven miles below sea level.

- **Seamounts** The ocean also features unusual forms we do not see on land. Pillars of rock and minerals stretch several stories high. Chimneys spout acid into the water. Seamounts, or underwater volcanoes, spew mud and gas into the sea.

GO ON →

- **Hydrothermal Vents** These holes on the ocean bottom eject material heated by the earth's core. Vents warm the surrounding waters from a chilly 37 degrees up to 392 degrees. In addition to the vents, the ocean contains hot springs that shoot out 650-degree water—hot enough to melt lead.

Strange Sea Creatures

4   Many of these unique habitats have alien-like creatures living there. Scientists have discovered 160-foot jelly creatures living around hydrothermal vents. Living near hot springs are 10-foot-tall tubeworms and giant clams. We have discovered life forms like these only recently. Many creatures have yet to be found. This makes sense because the ocean is Earth's largest habitat.

5   Many of these creatures live at the greatest depths, which pose the most dangers to human divers. Some, like the frilled shark, may hold clues to our planet's past. Measuring more than 5 feet long, the frilled shark swims about 5,000 feet below the surface. Scientists include this creature in a group called "living fossils"—animals similar to those who swam the seas during the time of the dinosaurs.

6   The deepest ocean-dweller discovered so far might be the fangtooth fish. Sometimes found only 6,500 feet down, its habitat extends to the icy waters 16,500 feet below the surface. The fangtooth may only be about 6 inches long, but it looks as scary as its name. Its long, pointed teeth are the largest of any other fish its size.

7   At 8 inches long, the creepy-looking Pacific viperfish has jagged teeth that look like needles. It swims 13,000 feet down into the darkness, luring its prey with luminous dots on its belly. Most creatures living deep in the ocean have a glow-in-the-dark feature. It can be used to communicate, to attract prey, or for defense. This feature is called *bioluminescence*, a chemical reaction within an organism that produces light.

8   Exploring the oceans may lead us to discover many new land forms and animals. Scientists also hope it will help us learn more about the planet, and even about ourselves. Studying hot springs and vents could help us discover new ways to produce energy. Other findings could lead to new medical treatments. We could also study creatures that survive in strange habitats—without heat, light, or oxygen. This could help us discover new ways to survive here on Earth—or even among the stars.

GO ON →

1 **Part A:** What does the word **luminous** mean as it is used in paragraph 7?

(A) deadly

(B) shining

(C) flashing

(D) poisonous

Part B: Which phrase from the paragraph helps the reader understand the meaning of **luminous**?

(A) "... luring its prey ..."

(B) "... used to communicate ..."

(C) "... chemical reaction ..."

(D) "... produces light ..."

GO ON →

2 **Part A:** Which sentence states the article's most important ideas?

Ⓐ The geography of our oceans contains many different features, some of which also appear on land.

Ⓑ Humans have worked to explore space because it is more appealing than the oceans on Earth.

Ⓒ To understand our planet, we must discover what lies beneath the waters that make up 70 percent of Earth.

Ⓓ Most of the strangest, fascinating creatures live in the deepest and darkest ocean habitats.

Part B: Select **two** sentences from the article that **best** support the answer in Part A.

Ⓐ "In the past 50 years, explorers have set their sights on the stars." (Paragraph 1)

Ⓑ "This 'world ocean' consists of the Pacific, our largest ocean, followed by the Atlantic, Indian, Southern, and Arctic Oceans." (Paragraph 2)

Ⓒ "Actually, the ocean bottom contains as many different features as our continents." (Paragraph 3)

Ⓓ "The ocean also features unusual forms we do not see on land." (Paragraph 3)

Ⓔ "Studying hot springs and vents could help us discover new ways to produce energy." (Paragraph 8)

Ⓕ "We could also study creatures that survive in strange habitats—without heat, light, or oxygen." (Paragraph 8)

GO ON →

Part A: Below are three points that the reader might infer from the article.

> **Points**
>
> Traveling into space is more appealing than exploring Earth's oceans.
>
> Studying species that inhabit alien-like ocean environments could help humans' future survival.
>
> The deeper a diver descends into the ocean, the more dangerous it becomes.

Circle the point that the author of the article supports with at least two pieces of evidence.

Part B: Underline **two** sentences from paragraph 8 that support the point selected in Part A.

> Exploring the oceans may lead us to discover many new land forms and animals. Scientists also hope it will help us learn more about the planet, and even about ourselves. Studying hot springs and vents could help us discover new ways to produce energy. Other findings could lead to new medical treatments. We could also study creatures that survive in strange habitats—without heat, light, or oxygen. This could help us discover new ways to survive here on Earth—or even among the stars.

GO ON →

4 Use information from "Oceans: Earth's Final Frontier" to summarize why scientists believe we should make a larger effort to explore the oceans.

Your essay should include details from the article about what explorers might find and the likely benefits of these discoveries.

Use the space below to plan your writing. Write your essay on a separate sheet of paper.

Read the article titled "Dive Technology" and answer the questions that follow.

Dive Technology

1   To explore the oceans, divers have to overcome hazards to human life. These include extreme darkness, freezing cold temperatures, and crushing water pressures. Through the years, inventors have tackled these challenges to make advances in underwater technology.

The Aqualung

2   In the 1940s, ocean explorer Jacques Cousteau helped invent the Aqualung. This device allowed divers to breathe under water. The Aqualung was a metal oxygen tank attached to a breathing tube that controlled the flow of oxygen. It was strapped with a harness to a diver's back. Scientists have since improved upon this invention, now known as SCUBA, for Self Contained Underwater Breathing Apparatus.

The Jim Suit

3   Even the most experienced scuba divers can go down only 130 feet for 10 minutes. To go beyond these limits, inventors created the Jim Suit. Based on astronauts' space suits, the Jim Suit protects wearers from deadly water pressure and contains built-in oxygen. In 1979, ocean scientist Sylvia Earle tested the Jim Suit in a record-breaking dive. She explored the ocean floor 1,250 feet below the surface for 2½ hours.

The Deepsea Challenger

4   In 2012, filmmaker James Cameron introduced his new invention: a one-person submarine called *The Deepsea Challenger*. Before, the deepest a submarine could travel was 4 miles down. Cameron broke this record when he took *The Deepsea Challenger* to the bottom of the Mariana Trench. Seven miles down, it is the deepest place on Earth.

5   Cameron's design is an example of advanced technology because it sits vertically in the water. This allows the sub to descend faster, rotating as it goes to keep it on course. *The Deepsea Challenger* has lights, 3-D cameras, and a scooper arm to collect samples. This revolutionary invention could transform ocean exploration.

GO ON →

5 **Part A:** What does the word **transform** mean as it is used in paragraph 5?

(A) make completely different

(B) go forward much faster

(C) make important

(D) turn expensive

Part B: Which word from the paragraph helps the reader understand the meaning of **transform**?

(A) example

(B) descend

(C) revolutionary

(D) invention

6 **Part A:** In what way is the Jim Suit better than the Aqualung?

(A) It allows divers to breathe under water.

(B) It allows divers to make longer, deeper dives.

(C) It allows divers to go down to the deepest place on Earth.

(D) It allows divers to rotate, take 3-D pictures, and collect samples.

Part B: Which detail **best** helps to explain how the Jim Suit is an improvement?

(A) It is based on astronauts' space suits.

(B) It is used by ocean scientists.

(C) It was invented after the Aqualung.

(D) It was tested by Sylvia Earle.

GO ON →

7 **Part A:** Which design element makes *The Deepsea Challenger* an improvement over other submarines?

(A) one-person seating

(B) a sample collector

(C) a vertical position

(D) bright lights

Part B: Select **two** sentences from the article that support the answer in Part A.

(A) "In 2012, filmmaker James Cameron introduced his new invention: a one-person submarine called *The Deepsea Challenger*." (Paragraph 4)

(B) "Before, the deepest a submarine could travel was 4 miles down." (Paragraph 4)

(C) "Cameron broke this record when he took *The Deepsea Challenger* to the bottom of the Mariana Trench." (Paragraph 4)

(D) "Cameron's design is an example of advanced technology because it sits vertically in the water." (Paragraph 5)

(E) "This allows the sub to descend faster, rotating as it goes to keep it on course." (Paragraph 5)

(F) "*The Deepsea Challenger* has lights, 3-D cameras, and a scooper arm to collect samples." (Paragraph 5)

GO ON →

Read the biography of James Cameron titled "Lights, Cameras, Invention!" and answer the questions that follow.

Lights, Camera, Invention!

1   In 2012, the only vehicle able to take people to the deep sea was almost 50 years old. What would it take to reinvent the submersible? As it turns out, a film director.

2   James Cameron is most famous for award-winning films such as *Titanic* and *Avatar*. He sometimes jokes that he makes blockbuster movies to support his passion for exploring the seas. His filmmaking fortune did help him fund his revolutionary invention: *The Deepsea Challenger*, a one-man **submersible**[1] that in 2012 traveled to the deepest place on Earth. However, Cameron's passion for ocean technology did not begin here.

3   In 1989, Cameron directed *The Abyss*, a science fiction movie in which characters traveled to the ocean depths. During filming, he introduced new ways of using cameras under water. Later, he controlled his robotic cameras inside the wreck of the sunken ship *Bismarck*. During the making of *Titanic*, Cameron made many dives to the wreck of the actual ship.

4   In this way, Cameron has been able to make films and advance underwater technology at the same time. He can use his ideas right away and study the results. Perhaps it is this combination of skill and creative thinking that has allowed Cameron to design submersibles in a new way.

5   With *The Deepsea Challenger*, Cameron has literally "upended" the design. Instead of traveling horizontally, his sub moves vertically, like a torpedo. This makes the ship much faster. He replaced the heavy steel shell with a lightweight foam structure. This allows the ship to rise quickly from the bottom. And he put the thrusters on the top, rather than the bottom. This prevents the craft from stirring up the seabed. Now the pilot (and cameras!) can clearly see the ocean floor.

---

submersible[1]—submarine

GO ON →

8 **Part A:** Which meaning of the word **craft** is used in paragraph 5?

(A) vehicle

(B) skill

(C) trickery

(D) occupation

Part B: Which word from the paragraph helps the reader understand the meaning of **craft**?

(A) design

(B) ship

(C) foam

(D) cameras

GO ON →

9 **Part A:** Which text structure used by the author of "Dive Technology" is not used by the author of "Lights, Cameras, Invention!"?

(A) chronology

(B) compare-and-contrast

(C) cause-and-effect

(D) categories

Part B: Which text element in "Dive Technology" supports the answer to Part A?

(A) words in italics

(B) subheadings

(C) transition sentences

(D) words in quotation marks

GO ON →

10 Organize the details that appear in "Dive Technology" and "Lights, Cameras, Invention!" by placing them into the correct box in the chart. Write all of the details in the chart.

Details:

The Deepsea Challenger can descend so quickly because of its vertical design.

Sylvia Earle holds the record for ocean exploration in a Jim Suit.

The Deepsea Challenger traveled to the deepest place on Earth.

James Cameron has used his films to test out new underwater technology.

Cameron has put some of his movie profits into funding underwater inventions.

Scuba diving equipment limits how deep divers can travel and how long they can stay under water.

Information in "Dive Technology" Only	
Information in Both Passages	
Information in "Lights, Cameras, Invention!" Only	

GO ON →

You have read three texts about ocean exploration. All three discuss challenges faced by ocean explorers. The three texts are:

- "Oceans: Earth's Final Frontier"

- "Dive Technology"

- "Lights, Cameras, Invention!"

Think about the information the authors provide to show how explorers are improving exploration under water.

Write an essay that describes challenges that explorers face in at least two of the texts. Tell how they can overcome those challenges through the use of underwater technology. Remember to use textual evidence to support your ideas.

Use the space below to plan your writing. Write your essay on a separate sheet of paper.

Narrative 1

Task:

Your class is learning about the adventure fiction genre. Your teacher has asked you to write an original adventure story. Before you write your story, you will read two adventures. You will also read an informational article that tells about the characteristics of adventure stories.

After you have reviewed these sources, you will answer some questions about them. Briefly scan the sources and the three questions that follow. Then, go back and read the sources carefully to gain the information you will need to answer the questions and write an original adventure story.

In Part 2, you will write an original adventure story using what you have learned from the two adventures and the informational article.

Directions for Part 1

You will now read two adventures and one article. You can re-examine any of the sources as often as you like.

Research Questions:

After reading the adventures and the article, use the remaining time in Part 1 to answer three questions about them. Your answers to these questions will be scored. Also, your answers will help you think about the sources you have read, which should help you write your own adventure story.

You may refer to the adventures and the article when you think it would be helpful. You may also refer to your notes. Answer the questions in the space provided..

GO ON →

Part 1

Source #1

The following scene is from a shipwreck that leaves the Robinson family stranded on a desert island.

adapted from
Swiss Family Robinson
by Johann David Wyss

We heard a loud cracking, as if the vessel was parting asunder; we felt that we were aground, and heard the captain cry, in a tone of despair, "We are lost! Launch the boats!"

These words were a dagger to my heart, and the lamentations of my children were louder than ever. I then recollected myself, and said, "Courage, my darlings, we are still above water, and the land is near. . . . Remain here, and I will endeavor to save us."

I went on deck, and was instantly thrown down, and wet through by a huge sea; a second followed. I struggled boldly with the waves, and succeeded in keeping myself up, when I saw, with terror, the extent of our wretchedness. The shattered vessel was almost in two; the crew had crowded into the boats, and the last sailor was cutting the rope. I cried out . . . but my voice was drowned in the roar of the tempest, nor could they have returned for us through waves that ran mountains high. . . .

I returned to my family, and endeavored to appear calm. "Take courage," cried I, "there is yet hope for us; the vessel, in striking between the rocks, is fixed in a position which protects our cabin above the water, and if the wind should settle tomorrow, we may possibly reach the land."

GO ON →

The Trap

It was evening when we met at the mouth of the river. I raised my shovel in acknowledgement, and I could see Milo's flashlight bobbing up and down on his forehead. Checking the torn map once more, I confirmed that this was the correct location.

"Eh! Ya sure now?" came Milo's voice from a few yards away, his flashlight still bobbing on his head.

"Yes," I hissed, trying not to lose patience with my assistant and his habit of questioning every move I made. "According to my calculations, the treasure is buried about 6 feet below this very spot."

Milo smiled a toothless grin and scratched his head. "Right then."

Taking a deep breath, I dug the shovel into the soft earth. Too late, I realized I had sprung a trap. Suddenly, the earth was disappearing around us and falling into a deep, dark crevice below. I scrambled for my footing and looked up to see Milo trip as he ran for cover. Desperately, he reached out to grab a hold of something, and I thrust my shovel at him while trying to gain an anchor for myself.

"I'm gonna fall!" he shouted through the noise of the rumbling earth as his entire weight dangled from the shovel.

I was ashamed to say I agreed with his prediction—that is, until I remembered the rope waiting by my backpack, not three feet away. Now if only I could find a way to reach it before the ground swallowed us whole!

GO ON →

Characteristics of an Adventure Story

Adventures are the most exciting stories found within the fiction genre. They are characterized by one word: ACTION! Regardless of where the characters are or what they're doing, there are sure to be many challenges to overcome that often involve risk, danger, and excitement.

The plotline of an adventure story typically revolves around a central hero or heroine. This character is almost always brave, strong, and quick-thinking. The hero or heroine has a certain code of honor, and this separates him or her from the rest of the characters. The hero also typically has a character flaw, such as arrogance. This helps the reader connect with the hero and root for him to improve over the course of the story. Often, there is also a sidekick who assists the hero and makes the story more interesting.

Almost every adventure story involves a journey or quest of some kind. The characters may be traveling through a strange jungle or desert, or perhaps they are on a quest for buried treasure. The journey itself is exciting, but the characters always face challenges along the way.

Adventure story characteristics include:

- Hero or heroine, possibly with a sidekick

- A journey or quest, often in a strange place

- Exciting action scenes that may involve danger

GO ON →

Research Questions

1 Which element specific to adventure stories do the excerpt from *Swiss Family Robinson* and "The Trap" have in common?

Ⓐ a quest across the ocean

Ⓑ exciting action that involves danger

Ⓒ heroes that have character flaws

Ⓓ sidekicks who make the story interesting

2 Describe how the information in the article helps you better understand both adventure stories. Support your answer with details from the article and the stories.

_____

_____

_____

_____

_____

GO ON →

3 Explain which parts of each of the three sources are most helpful for someone who must write an original adventure. Support your answer with details from the article and the stories.

_____

_____

_____

_____

_____

_____

_____

_____

_____

_____

_____

_____

_____

_____

GO ON →

Directions for Part 2

You will now look at the two adventures and the article, take notes, and plan, draft, revise, and edit your original adventure story. You may use your notes and go back to the sources. Now read your assignment and the information about how your adventure story will be scored; then begin your work.

Your assignment:

The two stories you read are examples of typical adventures. Write your own adventure story that is several paragraphs long and includes the characteristics of adventures discussed in the article and shown in the stories you read. Make sure to include narrative strategies such as dialogues, descriptions, characters, plot, setting, and closure. Be sure to develop your story completely.

REMEMBER: A well-written adventure story:

- has a plot filled with exciting action and possibly danger
- has a brave hero or heroine and possibly a sidekick
- involves a journey or quest
- has a beginning, middle, and end
- uses dialogues and descriptions
- follows rules of writing (spelling, punctuation, and grammar)

Now begin work on your adventure story. Manage your time carefully so that you can

1. plan your adventure
2. write your adventure
3. revise and edit the final draft of your adventure

For Part 2, you are being asked to write an original adventure story that is several paragraphs long. Write your response on a separate sheet of paper. Remember to check your notes and your prewriting/planning as you write and then revise and edit your adventure story.

Narrative 2

Student Directions

Task:

The Great Pyramid of Giza is the oldest and largest of the three pyramids that now stand in the city of Giza, in Egypt. The Great Pyramid is one of the Seven Wonders of the Ancient World because of its impressive size and how it was constructed.

For this task, you will be writing a narrative related to the topic of the Great Pyramid of Giza. Before you write your narrative, you will read two articles that provide information about the city and pyramids of Giza.

After you have reviewed these sources, you will answer some questions about them. Briefly scan the sources and the three questions that follow. Then, go back and read the sources carefully to gain the information you will need to answer the questions and write a narrative.

In Part 2, you will write a narrative on a topic related to the sources.

Directions for Part 1

You will now look at two sources. You can look at either of the sources as often as you like.

Research Questions:

After looking at the research sources, use the remaining time in Part 1 to answer three questions about them. Your answers to these questions will be scored. Also, your answers will help you think about the research sources you have read, which should help you write your narrative.

You may refer to the sources when you think it would be helpful. You may also refer to your notes. Answer the questions in the space provided.

GO ON →

The Ancient City of Giza

The city of Giza in Egypt holds many secrets of what life was like thousands of years ago. This highly organized city, often referred to as "The Lost City," is buried near the area where three famous pyramids of Giza stand today, the most famous being the Great Pyramid. Archaeologists have been digging up pieces of information for many years. They have discovered what life was like for some ancient Egyptians. It appears that Giza was mainly occupied during the years in which the pyramids were being built there. It is therefore believed that this city was home to the Egyptians who built these pyramids.

An area of the city was dedicated to housing the workers. This area was called "the galleries." It is where the workers slept, cooked, and spent any free time they had. The workers slept in military style. There were long bed platforms where the men would have slept, one right next to the other. They did not have separate living quarters. Hundreds, possibly thousands, of workers all lived together in these galleries.

The Egyptian workers seem to have been fed quite well. Bakeries and other food establishments have been discovered. Bread was a large part of their diet. They also enjoyed beef and fish.

Archaeologists have also made an important discovery about who the workers were. Previously, they had thought that slaves of the pharaohs built the pyramids. But evidence suggests that people came from many different parts of Egypt willingly to help build the pyramids for their pharaoh, whom they were eager to serve. They put in a certain amount of time working, possibly a few weeks or months, and then returned to their own homes.

Without these workers, the pyramids of Giza could have never been built. Their dedication and skill are forever seen in the ancient structures that still stand today.

GO ON →

The Great Pyramid: Giza's Ancient Wonder

Thousands of years ago, pharaohs ruled the land of Egypt. These ancient kings were worshipped by their people. Impressive pyramids were built to be the final resting place for the pharaohs and their families upon their death. Amazingly, many of these same pyramids still stand today. One example of such a structure, standing proudly above the rest, is the Great Pyramid of Giza.

Giza's Great Pyramid is one of the Seven Wonders of the Ancient World. It is an honor that is well deserved. This incredible pyramid is the oldest of the Seven Wonders, and it is also the only one that still stands today. For thousands of years, the Great Pyramid of Giza stood as the tallest man-made structure in the world. The largest pyramid ever built, it rises roughly 480 feet and consists of about 2 million enormous limestone blocks.

It took the people of Egypt decades to construct this pyramid for Pharaoh Khufu, who lived more than 4,500 years ago. Moving the blocks into place to build the pyramid was very difficult. Each block weighed between 2.5 and 15 tons. Archaeologists still disagree about how the workers managed to move them, sometimes from hundreds of miles away. Most scientists believe that sleds, ramps, and levers were used to position the stones around the base and up the pyramid. The ancient methods were not all that different from construction methods used today.

More than 100 pyramids have been discovered in Egypt. These amazing structures are a constant reminder of what the people of Egypt achieved thousands of years ago. And there is no better example of the architecture, planning, and skills of ancient Egyptians than the Great Pyramid of Giza.

GO ON →

Research Questions

1 How do you know that the Great Pyramid of Giza was a difficult structure to build? Provide two specific reasons from each source.
Be sure to name each source.

_____

_____

_____

_____

_____

2 What does the information in both sources suggest about the people of Egypt?

(A) They wanted to honor their pharaoh.

(B) They were forced to work hard day and night.

(C) They built many more pyramids than we know.

(D) They took longer than necessary to complete projects.

GO ON →

3 Which source provides the most useful information for a narrative that tells what life was like for a pyramid builder in ancient Giza? Provide two reasons for choosing this source.

_____

_____

_____

_____

GO ON →

Directions for Part 2

You will now look at your sources, take notes, and plan, draft, revise, and edit your narrative. You may use your notes and go back to the sources. Now read your assignment and the information about how your narrative will be scored; then begin your work.

Your assignment:

Your history club is researching ancient Egypt and how the pyramids were built. You have decided to write a multi-paragraph narrative that describes daily life for an Egyptian pyramid builder. In your narrative, you will write about a day in ancient Egypt from the point of view of a worker who is building the Great Pyramid of Giza. Your narrative will be read by members of your history club. In your narrative, include strategies such as dialogues, descriptions, characters, plot, setting, and closure.

REMEMBER: A well-written narrative:

- uses details from the sources to support the plot
- uses details from the sources to create characters
- uses details from the sources to describe the setting
- has a beginning, middle, and end
- uses dialogues and descriptions
- follows rules of writing (spelling, punctuation, and grammar)

Now begin work on your narrative. Manage your time carefully so that you can

1. plan your narrative
2. write your narrative
3. revise and edit the final draft of your narrative

For Part 2, you are being asked to write a narrative that is several paragraphs long. Write your response on a separate sheet of paper. Remember to check your notes and your prewriting/planning as you write and then revise and edit your narrative.

Opinion 1

Student Directions

Task:

The bottled water industry makes millions of dollars every year. Many people choose to purchase and drink bottled water every day. They do so knowing that other options, such as purified tap water, are readily available. Is bottled water the best choice for consumers to make?

For this task, you will be writing an opinion article related to the topic of bottled water. Before you write your article, you will review three sources that provide information about the bottled water industry and give opposing viewpoints about whether or not people should drink bottled water.

After you have reviewed these sources, you will answer some questions about them. Briefly scan the sources and the three questions that follow. Then, go back and read the sources carefully to gain the information you will need to answer the questions and write an article.

In Part 2, you will write an opinion article on a topic related to the sources.

Directions for Part 1

You will now read several sources. You can re-examine any of the sources as often as you like.

Research Questions:

After reading the research sources, use the remaining time in Part 1 to answer three questions about them. Your answers to these questions will be scored. Also, your answers will help you think about the research sources you have read, which should help you write your opinion article.

You may refer to the sources when you think it would be helpful. You may also refer to your notes. Answer the questions in the space provided.

GO ON →

The Bottled Water Industry: A Real Goldmine

The bottled water industry is certainly one to watch. Billions of dollars are spent on bottled water every year. And this industry appears to be growing more powerful around the world.

Every year, people drink more and more bottled water because of its convenience. Studies have shown that people in America buy and drink more bottled water than people in other countries; however, more and more people in other countries are increasing the amount of bottled water they consume. The industry as a whole is growing 10% each year, which means if 100 people bought bottled water last year, then 110 people will buy it this year. That is a huge increase in sales in a relatively short period of time.

In 2011, a study showed that a total of 9.1 billion gallons of bottled water was sold in the United States. If you break that number down, it comes out to almost 30 gallons of bottled water for each person. That means that, on average, every single person in the country drank four bottles of water each week for the whole year—and these numbers are expected to grow. That's a lot of bottled water that people are drinking!

What makes this industry so interesting? One reason is the fact that people are spending a lot of money on something that they can essentially get for free. Bottled water companies are making huge profits selling a product to people who can get it simply by turning on their faucet. Why? This question causes many debates. People have different opinions about the bottled water industry. But one thing we can all agree on is that bottled water is sold practically everywhere, and people are buying it. It looks like the demand for this product is here to stay.

GO ON →

Bottled Water: The Right Choice

Bottled water is a subject about which people have very different opinions. Some argue that bottling water is a bad idea. But the reality is that bottles of water are being sold everywhere and people continue to buy them. People see the benefits of bottled water; it is a wise alternative to tap water.

One of the biggest advantages of bottled water is the convenience of it. It is important for people to drink plenty of water throughout the day to stay healthy. It becomes even more important to drink water when you exercise or play sports. One rule of thumb is that people tend to drink more water if they are able to get it easily.

It is easy to grab a bottle of water before you leave the house so that you have it with you on your way to school. And taking a bottle of water and putting it in your gym bag on your way to a workout will help make sure that you have enough water while you exercise. Likewise, if you are thirsty and looking at options in a vending machine, a bottle of water offers a healthy choice to quench your thirst.

Many people feel that bottled water also tastes much better than tap water. Each brand of bottled water has a consistently good taste to it, but tap water tastes different depending on where it comes from. Different factors may cause tap water to taste better or worse to different people. Variances in tap water can be a problem when you are in different and unfamiliar places. How do you know how the tap water will taste? How do you know if it is clean enough? Bottled water will always taste the same wherever you buy it.

Another advantage of bottled water is that it can be shipped and stored easily. Sometimes natural events will cause the water supply to become damaged. When this happens, people will not be allowed to drink the water. Because water can be shipped so easily, getting clean water to the people who are affected can be done quickly. When a storm is coming that may cause us to lose electricity for a while, it is important to have enough clean water. We are actually told to have at least a three-day supply of water for each person. One gallon per person per day is the recommended amount. Buying a few cases of bottled water is simple enough to do to be prepared.

People will continue to have their own opinions about bottled water; however, it is hard to deny that some real benefits come from this product that many of us enjoy on a daily basis.

GO ON →

Bottled Water: The Wrong Choice

People all over the world buy bottled water, mainly because it is convenient to do so. Although bottled water does have some conveniences, it also comes with some harmful effects. These negative effects are not worth the ease of purchasing a bottle of water.

First, the bottle that holds the water needs to be made. The process of creating the plastic bottle is actually quite damaging to the environment. We are living in a time when we are all trying our best to limit the greenhouse effect and reduce our use of fossil fuels. The amount of fuel used to run the machines that are making the bottles is tremendous. Then even more fuel is being used by the trucks to deliver the bottles of water all over the world. This is not helping our efforts to reduce our use of fossil fuels.

Then, what do people do with their plastic bottles when they are finished drinking the water? Unfortunately, not enough people are recycling. A study showed that only one out of every six plastic bottles is recycled by Americans. The other five bottles are going to our already-overflowing landfills, where they will sit for years to come, taking up more of our land. It is believed that the people in our country add 24 billion plastic bottles each year to landfills. That is just terrible!

What makes this entire process even more terrible is the fact that we have access to clean, tasty water right in our own homes. Many people incorrectly believe that bottled water is cleaner than tap water. This is actually not true. The water that comes from your sink at home has gone through many different treatments and tests. Water companies are required to follow strict rules to make sure the tap water does not have anything in it that would harm us. Bottled water companies do not have to follow those same strict rules. As a result, the water in the bottles that we pay for may actually contain things that might be harmful to us.

And then there is the matter of the consumer cost of bottled water. It is true that tap water is not free. But although we must pay to have running water in our house, the difference in the cost of bottled water compared to tap water is huge. About 450 gallons of tap water costs the same as just one bottle of water.

The damage to our environment, the possible health risks, and the cost all greatly outweigh the convenience of bottled water. It is time to start filling your washable water bottle with tap water and stop buying bottled water.

GO ON →

Name: _____ Date: _____

Research Questions

1 Why might people choose to drink bottled water rather than tap water? Provide specific reasons from at least two sources in your answer. Be sure to name each source.

_____

_____

_____

_____

_____

2 Which information is repeated in all three sources?

(A) Bottled water is expensive.

(B) Bottled water is unnecessary.

(C) Bottled water is convenient.

(D) Bottled water is misunderstood.

GO ON →

3 Which of the three sources would be the most useful in making an argument for improving the quality of bottled water? Explain why, and support your answer with at least two details from that source.

_____

_____

_____

_____

_____

_____

_____

_____

_____

_____

_____

_____

_____

_____

_____

_____

GO ON →

Directions for Part 2

You will now look at your sources, take notes, and plan, draft, revise, and edit your article. You may use your notes and go back to the sources. Now read your assignment and the information about how your opinion article will be scored; then begin your work.

Your assignment:

Your school is considering adding an improved water purification system and removing all bottled water vending machines. As the editor of your school newspaper, you would like to write a multi-paragraph article giving your opinion about this decision. In your article, you will take a side as to whether you think the decision is a good one or whether it should be reconsidered. Your article will be read by the teachers and students at your school. In your article, clearly state your opinion and support your opinion with reasons that are thoroughly developed using information from what you have read.

REMEMBER: A well-written opinion article:

- has a clear opinion
- is well-organized and stays on the topic
- has an introduction and a conclusion
- uses transitions
- uses details from the sources to support your opinion
- develops ideas clearly
- uses clear language
- follows rules of writing (spelling, punctuation, and grammar)

Now begin work on your opinion article. Manage your time carefully so that you can

1. plan your article
2. write your article
3. revise and edit the final draft of your article

For Part 2, you are being asked to write an article that is several paragraphs long. Write your response on a separate sheet of paper. Remember to check your notes and your prewriting/planning as you write and then revise and edit your article.

Opinion 2

Student Directions

Task:

Many people show that they are committed to a community by helping to improve it in some way. This may involve projects that improve the structures and programs in the community. It may also involve volunteer opportunities that help people or animals in the community.

For this task, you will be writing an opinion article related to the topic of community service. Before you write your article, you will review three sources that provide information about how people can volunteer in their community and give opposing viewpoints about whether students should be required to do community service to graduate.

After you have reviewed these sources, you will answer some questions about them. Briefly scan the sources and the three questions that follow. Then, go back and read the sources carefully to gain the information you will need to answer the questions and write an article.

In Part 2, you will write an opinion article on a topic related to the sources.

Directions for Part 1

You will now read several sources. You can re-examine any of the sources as often as you like.

Research Questions:

After reading the research sources, use the remaining time in Part 1 to answer three questions about them. Your answers to these questions will be scored. Also, your answers will help you think about the research sources you have read, which should help you write your opinion article.

You may refer to the sources when you think it would be helpful. You may also refer to your notes. Answer the questions in the space provided.

GO ON →

Community Service

Contributing time to your community is effort well spent. There are many things you could do. Lending a helping hand to someone in need does a lot of good. Visiting people who are lonely will brighten both their day and yours. Most towns have different kinds of community service activities. You can usually find an activity that involves something you enjoy.

Senior centers and nursing homes often welcome the kindness of volunteers. You could entertain the elderly with a formal show that your dance school put together, or you could just stop by for a quick visit to say hello. Either way, senior citizens appreciate the effort.

Also, animal shelters are always in need of volunteers to help with the animals. Taking the dogs out for a walk or freshening up a few cages can make a big difference. Animal lovers are sure to find a useful way to spend some of their free time here.

Most of us already pitch in to help take care of the environment. As we all know, recycling is important and necessary, but there is so much more that you could do to improve the area you live in. You could clean up a local beach that you often go to. Another idea is putting some fresh paint on a nearby historical site, or planting flowers there; your work is sure to help make it a nicer place to visit.

The key is volunteering for something about which you feel passionate. Participating in a community service project that is close to your heart can be a very rewarding experience. When you look into which project to participate in, you are sure to be able to find one that will spark your interest.

GO ON →

Students Should Give Back to Their Communities

There are so many different ways that people could give back to their communities. Volunteering to participate in a community service project is one of those ways. Every neighborhood needs people to help with getting things done. Many school districts across the country have decided to have their students do their part as members of the community. They now require that their students volunteer a certain number of community service hours each year. Putting this idea into effect makes everyone a winner.

It is common for young people to not completely appreciate all that they may have. Participating in a community service project can change the way students view things. For example, volunteering to clean up a public park would help students realize that it takes hard work to keep that park looking nice and clean. The next time they drop a napkin or wrapper on the ground, they might think twice before leaving it there. They would know that someone else would have to pick it up if they did not. We are all able to better appreciate the things we have when we see how life would be without them.

Having students choose a volunteer project that means something to them is very important. Feeling a connection to the project would increase their interest in it. A student may be thinking that he or she would like a career in medicine. Volunteering at a local hospital might help the student determine if this is the right career choice. This opportunity would give the student hands-on experience in a field of interest.

It is possible that students might not have had the chance to volunteer on a community project until now. They might not have known how to find a program, or they might have been nervous to volunteer on their own. Groups of friends can now participate together in the same project. The school would be able to guide them on how to choose a program that is right for them. One great hope for this requirement is to give students a positive experience with volunteering. This would inspire students to continue volunteering throughout their lives, making a difference for years to come.

The decision to include community service as part of the regular school requirements is the right one. Obviously the community would benefit with more volunteers to help with the projects that need to be completed. In addition, students would have the chance to learn through real life experiences. Not everything can be taught in a classroom or from a book. Sometimes the best way to learn is to do.

GO ON →

Volunteering Should Be Voluntary!

Participating in a community service project is a wonderful way to spend your time. It shows that you feel connected to a certain cause in a strong way. It also shows that you are willing to work hard to help that cause. Unfortunately, this isn't always true for everyone who volunteers for a community service project. Some school districts require that their students volunteer a certain number of hours to a community service project. It is true that there is a positive side to having the students do this, but there are also negatives to consider.

When someone volunteers to do something, it should be for the right reasons. Volunteering means that you agree to help another person or cause for free. When students are required to be involved in community service so that they receive school credit, the schools are effectively taking away the true meaning of volunteering. In these situations, students may easily start to develop bad feelings about the whole experience. This may cause them to decide not to volunteer again in the future. The help the community receives would be temporary, but the lasting negative effects for the students could be permanent. This is surely not what the school would want to happen.

What about students who are truly committed to volunteering their time? When they apply to college, they include on their application the time they spent volunteering. This has always been viewed by colleges in a positive way. It shows that these students wanted to give back to their community. If the students volunteered because they had to, should colleges look at the time they spent helping others in the same way? Colleges will need to examine this dilemma as more and more schools begin to require community service.

Another factor to consider is whether students have time in their busy lives to take on community service. Many students are involved in after-school sports or music programs. These commitments already require that the students juggle homework, research projects, and extracurricular activities. Giving them the additional responsibility of community service hours may not be appropriate. Filling every minute of every day with an activity is too much to ask of anyone, and it is not a healthy way to live. Students who are required to volunteer may find their grades slipping or need to drop an after-school activity. Is having a community service requirement worth those risks?

Being a part of a community service project can bring many people a lot of joy. However, students need to realize and experience that on their own. Forcing it upon students is not the way to make them appreciate the good that volunteering really can accomplish.

GO ON →

Research Questions

1 What positive aspects of volunteering are presented in the sources?
Provide specific details from at least two sources in your answer.
Be sure to name each source.

_____

_____

_____

_____

_____

_____

_____

2 Which evidence in the second source best supports the opinion that
students should be required to volunteer in their community? Support
your answer with at least two details from the source.

_____

_____

_____

_____

_____

_____

_____

GO ON →

3 Which detail in the third source does NOT directly support the idea that students should not be required to perform community service?

(A) Being forced to volunteer may cause students to dislike community service.

(B) Colleges will need to consider how to view students with volunteer experience.

(C) Many students already have busy lives with after-school activities.

(D) Students should be allowed to seek out community projects on their own.

GO ON →

Directions for Part 2

You will now look at your sources, take notes, and plan, draft, revise, and edit your article. You may use your notes and go back to the sources. Now read your assignment and the information about how your opinion article will be scored; then begin your work.

Your assignment:

Your school is considering adding a community service requirement in order for students to graduate. As your class president, you would like to write a multi-paragraph article giving your opinion about this decision. In your article, you will take a side as to whether community service should be required or not. Your article will be read by the teachers and students at your school. In your article, clearly state your opinion and support your opinion with reasons that are thoroughly developed using information from what you have read.

REMEMBER: A well-written opinion article:

- has a clear opinion
- is well-organized and stays on the topic
- has an introduction and a conclusion
- uses transitions
- uses details from the sources to support your opinion
- develops ideas clearly
- uses clear language
- follows rules of writing (spelling, punctuation, and grammar)

Now begin work on your opinion article. Manage your time carefully so that you can

1. plan your article
2. write your article
3. revise and edit the final draft of your article

For Part 2, you are being asked to write an article that is several paragraphs long. Write your response on a separate sheet of paper. Remember to check your notes and your prewriting/planning as you write and then revise and edit your article.

Informational

Student Directions

Task:

One hundred and fifty years ago, huge distances separated the states and territories of our country. Long travel times made it hard to unite the nation. A new and faster form of travel was necessary; the solution was the Transcontinental Railroad.

For this task, you will be writing an informational article related to the topic of the Transcontinental Railroad, which united the eastern and western part of the United States in the 1800s. Before you write your article, you will review three sources that provide information about the Transcontinental Railroad, the workers who laid the tracks for it, and one of the people in charge of the project.

After you have reviewed these sources, you will answer some questions about them. Briefly scan the sources and the three questions that follow. Then, go back and read the sources carefully to gain the information you will need to answer the questions and write an article.

In Part 2, you will write an informational article on a topic related to the sources.

Directions for Part 1

You will now read several sources. You can re-examine any of the sources as often as you like.

Research Questions:

After reading the research sources, use the remaining time in Part 1 to answer three questions about them. Your answers to these questions will be scored. Also, your answers will help you think about the research sources you have read, which should help you write your informational article.

You may refer to the sources when you think it would be helpful. You may also refer to your notes. Answer the questions in the space provided.

GO ON →

Full Steam Ahead:
The Transcontinental Railroad

On July 4, 1870, a Boston trade official named Alex H. Rice stood on a San Francisco beach. In his hand was a bottle of water from the Atlantic Ocean that he had brought from the East Coast. At a signal from one of the other officials present on this historic day, Rice poured the water into the Pacific Ocean. This ceremony, called "the mingling of the waters," celebrated what had occurred less than a year before: the completion of the Transcontinental Railroad.

Connecting the two coasts by rail was one of the most important building projects in U.S. history. It turned a collection of states and territories into a united whole, and transformed the nation.

People had been asking for coast-to-coast rail travel for decades. Since the invention of the steam locomotive in 1825, companies had built many rail lines. These railroads connected eastern cities and seaports, slashing travel times and helping these areas grow. Crossing the country, however, was much more difficult. People and trade goods traveled by horse, stagecoach, or wagon train. The trip took months. Not many made the journey.

While the East became crowded, the West remained a wild frontier. People knew, however, that this half of the country was rich in resources. Land was plentiful and perfect for farming. Precious metals lay beneath the earth. Time and distance put these resources out of reach. Government and business leaders believed that where trains traveled, cities and businesses would sprout like corn. In 1862, Congress finally passed the Pacific Railroad Bill, a law that funded railroad companies and granted them land on which to build rails coast to coast.

Two companies immediately got to work. Railroads already existed that stretched from the East to Omaha, Nebraska. Now, the Union Pacific Railroad began extending the tracks from Omaha out to the West. The Central Pacific Railroad began in Sacramento, California and laid tracks to the East. Eventually, the two companies would meet in Promontory, Utah.

It was hard, backbreaking work that required lots of manpower. The Union Pacific hired Irish immigrants and Civil War veterans to do the job. The Central Pacific hired thousands of workers from China. Laying track westward meant blasting tunnels through the Rocky Mountains. The eastward route took the rails through the Sierra Nevada Mountains. Workers from both companies dangled from rocky slopes, hacking holes and placing explosives.

GO ON →

The workers also faced attacks from Native American tribes who lived on lands that were being gobbled up by the tracks. These peoples feared that the railroad would end their way of life.

Laying track was made even more dangerous by the competition between the two companies. The faster they laid track, the more money they earned. A faster pace also made working conditions more dangerous. Yet most workers earned only about $30 per month. Their efforts made it possible for the railroad to be completed seven years ahead of schedule.

On May 10, 1869, the rails were finally joined in Promontory at the "Golden Spike" ceremony. The final spike, made of gold, was tapped in, and engines driven from east and west met on the tracks. The transcontinental railroad was complete. The nation was about to move forward at top speed.

GO ON →

The Chinese Who Laid the Rails

It was 1865, and the Central Pacific Railroad Company had a problem. It needed 4,000 men to lay tracks for the eastbound section of the Transcontinental Railroad. Yet the company could only keep about 800 men on the job. Laying track was tough work performed at an exhausting pace. Workers also risked their lives blasting tunnels through mountains.

Contractor Charles Crocker wanted to hire workers from China. Many of these workers were already here. Chinese peasants had begun arriving in California in 1850. With poverty in their homeland and no chance to earn a living, they had fled across the Pacific. They worked in the mines at the height of the Gold Rush. Later, some became fishermen or servants to the wealthy. Competition over jobs led some Californians to resent the Chinese.

Crocker's foreman distrusted the Chinese and refused to hire them to build the railroad. Then a group of Irish immigrant railroad workers began fighting for higher wages. When they heard that Chinese workers might replace them, they backed down. The Central Pacific officials saw that fear over losing their jobs would make workers settle for less. Now the company went all out to hire Chinese workers. It even advertised in China. By 1868, the Chinese represented 80 percent of the workforce.

The railroad was impressed with how hard the Chinese worked. The men were well organized and met deadlines. Yet, they were still treated unfairly. Chinese workers received only $30 per month and no food or housing. In contrast, other railroad workers received $35 per month as well as housing.

GO ON →

Railman Charles Crocker

In 1849, an Indiana man named Charles Crocker headed for California. After crossing the Platte Valley in a wagon train, he made it to Sacramento. Crocker didn't know it at the time, but he had just traveled the future route of the Transcontinental Railroad.

In California, Crocker first worked the mines. Then he became a dry goods merchant. His business success caught the attention of the newly formed Central Pacific Railroad. Impressed with his intelligence and commitment, the company gave Crocker its first construction contract.

Crocker had no actual construction experience. So he hired an experienced team to lay the first 18 miles of track. As they worked, Crocker rode along, watching and learning. After taking over the job, his smartest move was hiring Chinese workers. This helped him overcome a severe labor shortage. It also became a key strategy in the competition with the Union Pacific, which laid the westbound track.

The more track each company laid, the more money it made. It was the Chinese men who succeeded in the dangerous, backbreaking work that took the railroad through the Sierra Nevada mountains. Crocker was proud of these accomplishments, and knew he could rely on his workers. After hearing the Union Pacific brag about how fast the company laid track, he decided to prove his own workers' worth. On April 20, 1869, his crews laid ten miles of track across the Utah desert. This put the Central Pacific less than ten miles from the westbound rails. This amazing feat became known as "Victory Day."

GO ON →

Research Questions

1 Which sentence in the third source is irrelevant to the idea that Charles Crocker helped to ensure the Transcontinental Railroad was completed?

(A) "Crocker had no actual construction experience."

(B) "So he hired an experienced team to lay the first 18 miles of track."

(C) "After taking over the job, his smartest move was hiring Chinese workers."

(D) "On April 20, 1869, his crews laid ten miles of track across the Utah desert."

2 What point of view is expressed in each passage? Provide one example from each source in your answer. Be sure to name each source.

_____

_____

_____

_____

_____

_____

_____

_____

GO ON →

3 Which source provides evidence that best describes the state of the nation during the first half of the nineteenth century? Support your answer with at least two details from the source.

_____

_____

_____

_____

_____

_____

_____

_____

_____

_____

_____

_____

_____

_____

_____

GO ON →

Directions for Part 2

You will now look at your sources, take notes, and plan, draft, revise, and edit your article. You may use your notes and go back to the sources. Now read your assignment and the information about how your informational article will be scored; then begin your work.

Your assignment:

Your class is studying westward expansion. Your teacher has asked you to write a multi-paragraph article explaining the purpose of the Transcontinental Railroad, the challenges the workers faced, and the results of the completed railroad. Your article will be read by the students in your class and your teacher. In your article, clearly state the main idea and support your main idea with details using information from what you have read.

REMEMBER: A well-written informational article:

- has a clear main idea
- is well-organized and stays on the topic
- has an introduction and a conclusion
- uses transitions
- uses details from the sources to support your main idea
- develops ideas clearly
- uses clear language
- follows rules of writing (spelling, punctuation, and grammar)

Now begin work on your informational article. Manage your time carefully so that you can

1. plan your article
2. write your article
3. revise and edit the final draft of your article

For Part 2, you are being asked to write an article that is several paragraphs long. Write your response on a separate sheet of paper. Remember to check your notes and your prewriting/planning as you write and then revise and edit your article.

End-of-Year Assessment

Read the poem "The Oak" and answer the questions that follow.

The Oak

1   For centuries the oak has stood, spreading toward the sky,
   its roots a tangled network far below.
   As generations prosper, it has watched them live and die,
   borne witness to Earth's steady ebb and flow.

5   It watched a street come speeding by from far beyond the hill,
   followed by a house—then two, then three.
   And when the oak grew taller it could see the textile mill
   and glimpse the sun a-glitter on the sea.

   Years grow into decades that turn homes into a town,
10 as avenues aplenty cross the green.
   The oak, too, branches out—becomes a thing of great renown
   that draws folk—young and old and in-between.

   Its oaken arms give shelter—storm or sun—it stands so tall,
   and soothes our every sorrow, pain, or grief.
15 And through the seasons' cycles, it rejuvenates us all
   through every green, red, brown, or golden leaf.

   Inside its trunk the years are circles, ring 'round every ring,
   like ripples from a rock tossed in a lake.
   The oak is old and withered now, some limbs are hollow things,
20 while others hang low, bending close to break.

GO ON →

For centuries the oak has stood, spreading toward the sky,

but now the people gather one last time

to sing songs in its honor and to speak a sad goodbye

as they hoist the children up for one last climb.

25   As wind wafts through its branches, singing one last sad salute,

the old oak senses something we all know:

Beside it, there's an acorn sending out its first green shoot,

to carry on Earth's steady ebb and flow.

1 **Part A:** What is the meaning of the word **ebb** as it is used in lines 4 and 28?

(A) low tide waters

(B) a falling away

(C) a loosening

(D) exhaustion

Part B: Which antonym for the word **ebb** can help the reader figure out the meaning in Part A?

(A) centuries

(B) network

(C) witness

(D) flow

GO ON →

2 **Part A:** Which sentence states the major theme of the poem?

(A) Trees show us the beauty of the seasons.

(B) All living things should be treated with respect.

(C) Life is a continuing cycle of birth, growth, and change.

(D) An oak tree can create a child's most vivid memories.

Part B: Select **two** lines from the poem that illustrate the theme from Part A.

(A) "its roots a tangled network far below" (Line 2)

(B) "As generations prosper, it has watched them live and die" (Line 3)

(C) "and glimpse the sun a-glitter on the sea" (Line 8)

(D) "Its oaken arms give shelter—storm or sun—it stands so tall" (Line 13)

(E) "and soothes our every sorrow, pain, or grief" (Line 14)

(F) "to carry on Earth's steady ebb and flow" (Line 28)

GO ON →

3 **Part A:** Which word describes the speaker's point of view in the poem?

(A) thoughtful

(B) gloomy

(C) excited

(D) opinionated

Part B: Which description of events in the poem results from the point of view in Part A?

(A) The speaker describes mostly sad or emotional events.

(B) The speaker describes many kinds of events over centuries.

(C) The speaker describes events important only to the townspeople.

(D) The speaker describes events from the oak tree's perspective only.

GO ON →

4 **Part A:** How does the poet structure the poem to represent the beginning and end of the oak tree?

(A) by using rhyming words in stanzas 1 and 7

(B) by repeating lines 1 and 4 later in the poem

(C) by describing the town's growth in stanzas 2 and 3

(D) by describing the oak tree's advanced age in lines 19 and 20

Part B: In what other way does the structure of the poem represent the passing of time?

(A) Each stanza represents a specific season or moment in time.

(B) Each stanza contains four lines to show the steady movement of time.

(C) The lines in each stanza follow the pattern "long, short, long, short" to echo the ebb and flow of time.

(D) The poem contains an uneven number of stanzas to show that time has a beginning, middle, and end.

5 Underline **two** lines from the last two stanzas below that convey a hopeful message about time.

For centuries the oak has stood, spreading toward the sky,
but now the people gather one last time
to sing songs in its honor and to speak a sad goodbye
as they hoist the children up for one last climb.

As wind wafts through its branches, singing one last sad salute,
the old oak senses something we all know:
Beside it, there's an acorn sending out its first green shoot,
to carry on Earth's steady ebb and flow.

→

93

Mary Bowser: Civil War Spy

1   Sometime in the late 1830s, a girl named Mary was born as a slave in Richmond, Virginia. She was to become one of the most effective spies in American history.

2   Mary was born on a plantation owned by John Van Lew. When he died, his wife and daughter Elizabeth freed the family's slaves. Mary decided to stay with the family as a servant. Taking note of Mary's exceptional intelligence, Elizabeth Van Lew sent her to the Quaker School for Negroes in Philadelphia. Here, Bowser learned to read and write—skills that would later serve her well.

3   After finishing school, Mary returned to Richmond, where on April 16, 1861 she married a free man named Wilson Bowser. The next day, Virginia seceded from the Union. The United States was on the brink of civil war. Mary Bowser's life was about to undergo a radical change.

4   Bowser had kept in touch with Elizabeth Van Lew, who supported the movement to abolish slavery. Van Lew led a ring of Union spies working to obtain secret information about the South's wartime plans. She arranged for Bowser to become a servant in the Confederate White House of Jefferson Davis. As a spy, Bowser became Ellen Bond, an illiterate slave.

5   Instantly, Bowser had access to secret meetings, troop movements, and political strategies. Assuming she was a dim-witted girl who could not read, no one thought to hide classified documents or shield their conversations. Bowser also had a photographic memory. Bowser's contact noted that Bowser could recite complete documents from memory. He and Bowser exchanged information by hiding notes in empty eggshells, shoe soles, and bakery deliveries.

6   Near the end of the Civil War, Confederate President Davis started to suspect he had a spy in his house. To avoid detection, Bowser left her position in January 1865. She went on to teach freed slaves.

GO ON →

6 **Part A:** What does the word **illiterate** mean as it is used in paragraph 4?

Ⓐ unable to hear

Ⓑ unable to read

Ⓒ obedient

Ⓓ loyal

Part B: Which type of clue to the meaning of **illiterate** does the author provide in paragraph 5?

Ⓐ definition

Ⓑ antonym

Ⓒ synonym

Ⓓ context

GO ON →

7 **Part A:** Which skill probably helped Mary Bowser go "under cover" as Ellen Bond?

(A) acting

(B) reading

(C) writing

(D) intelligence

Part B: How did Bower use the skill in Part A?

(A) to memorize documents

(B) to listen in on meetings

(C) to appear dim-witted

(D) to write secret notes

GO ON →

8 **Part A:** What caused Elizabeth Van Lew to send Bowser to school in Philadelphia?

(A) She freed all of her father's slaves.

(B) She supported the abolition of slavery.

(C) She wanted Bowser to become a Union spy.

(D) She noticed that Bowser was highly intelligent.

Part B: Which of the following were a direct result of Bowser's education? Write **two** sentences in the Effects column of the graphic organizer.

Sentences:

She was hired as a servant in the Confederate White House.

She read classified documents.

She listened in on secret meetings.

She had a photographic memory.

She changed her name to Ellen Bond.

She wrote notes about information she had gathered.

Cause	Effects
Bowser's Education	

GO ON →

9 **Part A:** Which phrase **best** states how Bowser is described in this passage?

(A) as a freed slave who took on a fake name and identity

(B) as a former slave who was freed by her master's daughter

(C) as a married woman who became a Civil War spy

(D) as an intelligent woman whose education allowed her to become an effective Civil War spy

Part B: Select **two** sentences from the passage that support the answer in Part A.

(A) "When he died, his wife and daughter Elizabeth freed the family's slaves." (Paragraph 2)

(B) "Here, Bowser learned to read and write—skills that would later serve her well." (Paragraph 2)

(C) "After finishing school, Mary returned to Richmond, where on April 16, 1861 she married a free man named Wilson Bowser." (Paragraph 3)

(D) "Bowser had kept in touch with Elizabeth Van Lew, who supported the movement to abolish slavery." (Paragraph 4)

(E) "Instantly, Bowser had access to secret meetings, troop movements, and political strategies." (Paragraph 5)

(F) "To avoid detection, Bowser left her position in January 1865." (Paragraph 6)

GO ON →

10 Which events in paragraphs 2 through 5 affected Bowser's ability to become a Union spy in the Confederate White House? Underline **one** sentence in each paragraph.

Mary was born on a plantation owned by John Van Lew. When he died, his wife and daughter Elizabeth freed the family's slaves. Mary decided to stay with the family as a servant. Taking note of Mary's exceptional intelligence, Elizabeth Van Lew sent her to the Quaker School for Negroes in Philadelphia. Here, Bowser learned to read and write—skills that would later serve her well.

After finishing school, Mary returned to Richmond, where on April 16, 1861 she married a free man named Wilson Bowser. The next day, Virginia seceded from the Union. The United States was on the brink of civil war. Mary Bowser's life was about to undergo a radical change.

Bowser had kept in touch with Elizabeth Van Lew, who supported the movement to abolish slavery. Van Lew led a ring of Union spies working to obtain secret information about the South's wartime plans. She arranged for Bowser to become a servant in the Confederate White House of Jefferson Davis. As a spy, Bowser became Ellen Bond, an illiterate slave.

Instantly, Bowser had access to secret meetings, troop movements, and political strategies. Assuming she was a dim-witted girl who could not read, no one thought to hide classified documents or shield their conversations. Bowser also had a photographic memory. Bowser's contact noted that Bowser could recite complete documents from memory. He and Bowser exchanged information by hiding notes in empty eggshells, shoe soles, and bakery deliveries.

GO ON →

Read "Patel's Chain of Adventures" and answer the questions that follow.

Patel's Chain of Adventures

1   Patel flicked on the lamp next to his bed, flooding the room with a warm orange glow. He was almost halfway through his new book—and he'd only checked it out from the library yesterday. He was lost in the pages when his mom appeared in the doorway.

2   "Patel, can you please take out the garbage?" she asked, leaning against the doorframe.

3   "Ugh, Mom. Now? I'm at a really cool spot in my book," Patel pleaded. "Can't I just take it out in the morning?"

4   "Alright," she said. "But don't forget. The truck comes at around eight."

5   Patel read a few more chapters, then turned out the light, his mind wandering from the book to tomorrow's plans. Alex had invited him and Oscar over after school to play his new spy video game. In "Undercover Adventures," you collected special gadgets and went on secret missions. Patel could hardly wait.

6   The next morning, Patel woke to the numbers 7:50 flashing red on his clock. He must have forgotten to set the alarm. Jumping out of bed, he hurried to the closet and threw on his clothes.

7   In the kitchen, chaos reigned. His sister Maya was toddling across the floor, crying. When she reached their dad, he scooped her up, bouncing her gently as he finished packing her lunchbox. Patel wiggled her little foot and made a funny face. Maya giggled.

8   "I was just about to wake you," said Patel's dad, grabbing his briefcase and Maya's lunchbox. "We'll, we're off to work and daycare—not necessarily in that order. Have a good day!"

9   As they left, his mother walked in yawning, still wearing her pajamas. "Patel!" she exclaimed suddenly. "Why is the trash still here?"

10   Patel felt a stone dropping in his stomach. When he looked out the window and saw that full trashcans still lined the sidewalk, his panic lifted.

11   "It's all cool, Mom," he said. "The truck didn't come yet." Then he heard an unmistakable rumble.

12   "The truck!" Patel yelled. He grabbed two tall black bags and ran out of the house. The truck was stopped right in front of his house. He ran faster, dragging the bags along the path. Just before he reached the sidewalk, one of the bags split, spewing a week's worth of garbage all over him.

GO ON →

13   "Eew, gross!" he wailed. A banana peel was sliding off his knee. His jeans were spotted in wet coffee grounds and he smelled like rotten lettuce. Sighing, Patel cleaned everything up and trudged back to the house. After telling his mom what happened, he washed up and changed his clothes. By the time he finished, he had missed the school bus.

14   "Come on," said his mom. "I'll drive you to school on my way to work."

15   Already tired, Patel melted into the passenger seat of his mom's little blue car. His mom turned the key and the car coughed. Then it sputtered, clicked, and died.

16   "The old girl needs a new battery," his mom said. "Come on. We'll call a cab."

17   Patel finally arrived at school fifteen minutes late. He would have to stay after school. And his bad luck wasn't over yet. In this morning's panic, he had forgotten his math homework—so Mr. Crane made him stay inside during recess.

18   When the bell finally rang at the end of the day, Patel watched Alex and Oscar head off without him. He would have to catch the late bus and miss out on "Undercover Adventures."

19   Later that night, Patel was back in bed with his library book. But his mind kept wandering. How could someone have so much bad luck in one day?

20   His mom appeared at his door. "Don't forget—tomorrow is picture day," she said. "Why don't you pick out what you want to wear, and lay your clothes out tonight?" She looked at his book and smiled. "Or, you could just do it in the morning."

21   "Oh, no," Patel said, shutting the book and heading for his bureau. He had just realized that bad luck was not responsible for today's "adventures." And he was not going to leave anything for the morning again.

GO ON →

11 **Part A:** Why does the author use the phrase **a stone dropping in his stomach** in paragraph 10?

(A) to describe Patel's alarm about forgetting the trash

(B) to describe Patel's hunger before breakfast

(C) to show Patel's hatred for taking out the trash

(D) to show how tired Patel feels in the morning

Part B: Which phrase from the passage helps the reader understand the meaning in Part A?

(A) ". . . walked in yawning . . ." (Paragraph 9)

(B) ". . . his panic lifted." (Paragraph 10)

(C) ". . . an unmistakable rumble." (Paragraph 11)

(D) ". . . dragging the bags. . ." (Paragraph 12)

GO ON →

12 **Part A:** Why does Patel want to put off taking out the trash at the beginning of the story?

(A) He dislikes handling garbage.

(B) He is excited about tomorrow's plans.

(C) He is involved in reading a book.

(D) He knows the truck arrives at eight o'clock.

Part B: Which of the following is directly caused by the delay in Part A?

(A) Maya cries in the kitchen.

(B) His mom's car won't start.

(C) Patel smells like wet coffee grounds.

(D) Patel hurries with the trash and spills it.

GO ON →

13 **Part A:** Why does Patel have to stay after school?

Ⓐ Patel forgets his math homework.

Ⓑ Patel misses the school bus.

Ⓒ Patel arrives fifteen minutes late.

Ⓓ Patel forgets that it is picture day.

Part B: What happens because Patel has to stay after school?

Ⓐ He misses the late bus home.

Ⓑ He misses out on "Undercover Adventures."

Ⓒ He forgets to bring home his library book.

Ⓓ He forgets to take out the garbage.

GO ON →

14 **Part A:** What can the reader infer about Patel from details in the story?

Ⓐ Patel is a responsible kid who sometimes forgets to plan ahead.

Ⓑ Patel is involved in so many activities that he resents having to do his chores.

Ⓒ Patel's interest in books and video games makes him neglect his schoolwork.

Ⓓ Patel's family responsibilities make it difficult for him to manage his activities.

Part B: Which statement about the story supports the answer in Part A?

Ⓐ Patel forgets to bring his math homework into school.

Ⓑ Patel begs his mother to let him take out the trash in the morning.

Ⓒ Patel fails to realize that delaying his chore will lead to other problems.

Ⓓ Patel is punished twice in one day by his teacher Mr. Crane.

GO ON →

15 **Part A:** Which word **best** describes Patel's reaction to the problems he experiences in the story?

(A) anger

(B) amazement

(C) frustration

(D) sadness

Part B: Which sentence from the story supports the answer in Part A?

(A) "Jumping out of bed, he hurried to the closet and threw on his clothes." (Paragraph 6)

(B) "Sighing, Patel cleaned everything up and trudged back to the house." (Paragraph 13)

(C) "Already tired, Patel melted into the passenger seat of his mom's little blue car." (Paragraph 15)

(D) "How could someone have so much bad luck in one day?" (Paragraph 19)

GO ON →

16 **Part A:** Which of the following **best** states the main theme of this story?

(A) Children should take more responsibility for household chores.

(B) Delaying responsibilities can have unexpected consequences.

(C) True friends will stick by each other even in difficult situations.

(D) Parents should be less willing to give into children's demands.

Part B: Which sentence from the passage supports the answer in Part A?

(A) "When she reached their dad, he scooped her up, bouncing her gently as he finished packing her lunchbox." (Paragraph 7)

(B) "'Patel!' she exclaimed suddenly. 'Why is the trash still here?'" (Paragraph 9)

(C) "When the bell finally rang at the end of the day, Patel watched Alex and Oscar head off without him." (Paragraph 18)

(D) "And he was not going to leave anything for the morning again." (Paragraph 21)

GO ON →

17 **Part A:** At first, how does Patel explain everything that happens to him in the story? Select one answer and write it in the **Before** box.

Explanations

He caused all the problems.

He is having bad luck.

He has too many chores.

His teacher is too strict.

```
┌─────────────────────────────────────┐
│                                     │
│  Before                             │
│                                     │
│                                     │
│                                     │
│                                     │
│                                     │
└─────────────────────────────────────┘
```

Part B: What does Patel learn by the end of the story? Select one answer and write it in the **After** box.

Lessons Learned

Bad luck can happen to anyone.

It's impossible to change what is bound to happen.

Patel himself is responsible for the series of events.

Patel's mom should remind him about things much earlier.

```
┌─────────────────────────────────────┐
│                                     │
│  After                              │
│                                     │
│                                     │
│                                     │
│                                     │
│                                     │
│                                     │
└─────────────────────────────────────┘
```

GO ON →

18 **Part A:** Recreate Patel's "chain of adventures" by writing the events in the chart in the correct sequence.

> **Events:**
>
> His mom's car won't start, so Patel is late to school.
>
> Patel misses out on playing "Undercover Adventures."
>
> Patel decides to put off taking out the trash until the next morning.
>
> Patel has to stay after school for being late.
>
> Patel has to hurry with the garbage and it spills all over him.
>
> Because Patel has to change his clothes, he misses the bus.

>

>

>

>

>

>

GO ON →

Now you will read two articles about animals and the interesting ways in which they interact with each other. The first text, "Animal Societies," gives information about some specific groups of animals that live in interesting ways. The second text, "Crow Families," provides information about how crows behave in their social groups.

As you read the texts, pay close attention to details in the pieces. You will answer questions about both texts.

Read "Animal Societies" and "Crow Families" and answer the questions that follow.

Animal Societies

1   What do bees, wolves, and naked mole-rats have in common? They are some of the many animals that live in social groups. Not every animal grouping is a society. Biologists say that social behavior has two qualities: **cooperation,** where animals interact in ways that benefit the whole group; and **division of labor,** where each group member has a specific job.

Living in Colonies

2   The most highly organized animal group is the colony. Usually, it is led by a queen—the only group member that can reproduce. All other residents know their place, and each is bred for one specific job.

3   Some colony residents seek out food. Others are builders that maintain the nest. Some stand guard and some feed the young. Life is so specialized that some biologists compare animal colonies to cells working together in a single body. The scientific term for species in these complex societies is **eusocial** animals.

Naked Mole-Rats

4   The majority of eusocial animals are insects living in colonies of thousands. One exception is a mammal called the naked mole-rat. Naked mole-rats live in the dry regions of Kenya, Ethiopia, and Somalia in underground colonies of 100–300 individuals. Yet only one female, along with one or two males, has the ability to breed. The rest work to maintain the burrow, or act as soldiers to defend against intruders.

5   Scientists believe that naked mole-rats developed this cooperative society as the best way to survive. Their major food source—roots and tubers—are scattered in small quantities and hidden under dry ground. Living in smaller groups would mean greater competition over scarce resources. That's why the naked mole-rat prefers living in large groups near a known food source.

GO ON →

Ants Everywhere

6   More than 12,000 species of ants live in colonies all over the world. Most residents are female, but only the queen can reproduce. Males are born only to mate. The other colony residents—which can number in the thousands—belong to either a worker or soldier caste.

7   The dangerous driver ant lives in tropical rain forests. Driver ants do not have a permanent nest. Instead, the entire colony moves as a single mass, eating everything in its path—insects, rodents, or even goats. Soldier ants with large, powerful jaws move along the outside. Ringing the inside are the worker ants, whose bodies protect the queen and larvae in the center.

The Meerkat Mob

8   Besides colonies, animal societies include other groups. Wolves live in packs that cooperate on the hunt. Elephants live in female-led herds in which all adults act as caretakers for the young. Dolphins live in pods where each individual has its own signature whistle.

9   A group of meerkats, called a *mob*, averages about 30 family members. A meerkat is a type of South African mongoose. Each mob digs several underground burrows. Each burrow contains a complicated tunnel-and-room system that stays cool even during the hottest days. Often, large burrows contain as many as 90 entrances.

10   A meerkat mob gives its members the benefits of social living. Meerkats seek out food as a group. Meanwhile, other mob members stand guard. These sentries look out for eagles, hawks, and other birds. Meerkats also care for young in teams, with both males and females taking turns babysitting the pups.

GO ON →

Crow Families

1   Have you ever seen a tree covered in black leaves? A closer looks reveals that the "leaves" are actually crows—hundreds of them. While this might seem creepy, these birds are simply hanging out with their extended family.

2   Crows belong to large social groups, sometimes containing thousands of birds. Scientists refer to a group of these birds as "a murder of crows." Each crow mates for life. This creates tight-knit families in which young crows help their parents care for younger siblings. Crow families even develop certain behaviors that can differ from one family to another.

3   One behavior called "anting" is passed down only in some crow families. These crows cover themselves in crushed ants. This action releases an acid that prevents parasites from burrowing into the birds' feathers.

4   Like most societies, flocks of crows compete for territory and resources. Some even steal each other's food. But social living makes crows highly intelligent and capable of preventing theft. For example, a crow will sometimes pretend to hide food in one location, but put it in another.

5   Playing is another social behavior. Crows play with each other by snatching or dropping objects. Or they fly high up, then tumble down with the wind. Crows also use tools. They crack nuts or shells open by dropping them onto a hard surface. They can even bend a piece of wire and use it to retrieve hard-to-get-at food.

6   Crows can also be highly selective. If a crow is excluded from a group, it might not be allowed to rejoin. Still, crows often work together to help their fellow crows. Crows communicate with 250 different types of calls. Upon hearing a distress call, crows will rush to protect another crow from an enemy.

GO ON →

Name: _____ **Date:** _____

Answer these questions about "Animal Societies."

19 In paragraph 1 of "Animal Societies," the author uses the phrase "division of labor" to describe the jobs of different group members. Write in the word web **five** words from the passage that belong to this category.

queen	residents	builders	cells	species	insects
mammals	workers	soldiers	packs	caretakers	pods
foragers	sentries				

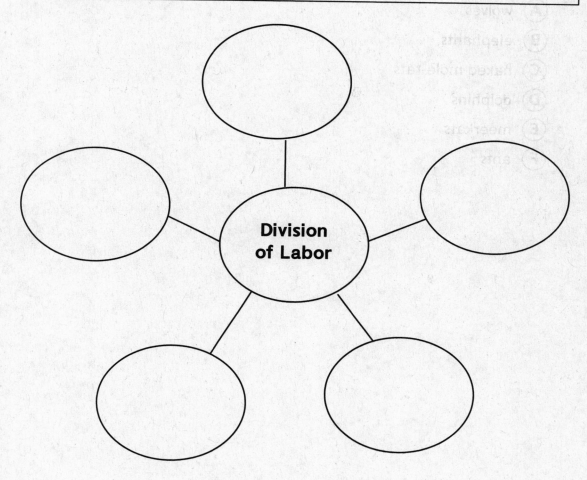

Division of Labor

20 **Part A:** How do biologists define eusocial animals?

(A) Those that live in underground colonies

(B) Large groups that live near a known food source

(C) Those that live in female-led groups of adult caretakers

(D) Specialized colonies where individuals work like cells in one body

Part B: Select **two** animals that are examples of eusocial animals.

(A) wolves

(B) elephants

(C) naked mole-rats

(D) dolphins

(E) meerkats

(F) ants

GO ON →

21 **Part A:** What is one behavior that separates social groups from other animal groups?

(A) reproduction

(B) cooperation

(C) communication

(D) hunting

Part B: What is the major purpose of social animal groups?

(A) to help animals recognize one another

(B) to produce better offspring

(C) to increase chances of survival

(D) to make permanent homes

GO ON →

Answer these questions about "Crow Families."

22 **Part A:** Which main factor has led to the crow's high intelligence?

(A) social living

(B) roosting in trees

(C) using tools

(D) playing in the wind

Part B: Select **two** examples of intelligent crow behavior.

(A) flocking with extended family

(B) mating for life

(C) using hard surfaces to crack open shells

(D) snatching up objects

(E) excluding other crows

(F) retrieving food with bent wire

GO ON →

Name: _____ Date: _____

23 Crows display specific characteristics. Complete the chart about crow families by writing in the correct box a result and an example for each characteristic in the chart.

Possible Results

competition for territory

excluding others

tight-knit families

distress calls

family-specific behaviors

Possible Examples

hiding of food

anting

bending wire

young help parents care for siblings

snatching or dropping of nuts

Crow Families		
Characteristic	**Result**	**Example**
mate for life		
adults pass on behaviors to young		

GO ON →

Now answer these questions about "Animal Societies" and "Crow Families."

24 **Part A:** What is similar about "Animal Societies" and "Crow Families"?

(A) They contain information about animal colonies.

(B) They contain information about eusocial animals.

(C) They contain information about animals that live underground.

(D) They contain information about animals that live in social groups.

Part B: How is the structure of "Animal Societies" different from that of "Crow Families"?

(A) "Animal Societies" compares and contrast different animal groups; "Crow Families" organizes information about crows in categories.

(B) "Animal Societies" lists information about animal groups in order of importance; "Crow Families" compares and contrasts information about crows with that of other animals.

(C) "Animal Societies" lists information about animal groups in categories; "Crow Families" organizes information about crows by causes and effects.

(D) "Animal Societies" describes problems and solutions of different animal groups; "Crow Families" organizes information about crows in chronological order.

GO ON →

25 Using information from both passages, write each type of animal in the correct box in the chart. One social group should contain two animal types.

Name of Social Group	Type of Animal
colony	
pack	
murder	
pod	
herd	
mob	

Animals

wolf

meerkat

elephant

crow

ant

dolphin

naked mole-rat

GO ON →

26 **Part A:** Based on information in both passages, what conclusion can the reader draw about social animals?

(A) Animals that live in underground colonies have a better chance of survival than other animal societies.

(B) Shared caretaking of the young benefits many animal societies by freeing adults to cooperate on other tasks.

(C) Excluding certain individuals from a social group is important to the survival of the greater society.

(D) All types of animal social groups do best when they contain a male/female pair that mates for life.

Part B: Select **one** sentence from each passage that supports the answer in Part A.

(A) "Usually, it is led by a queen—the only group member that can reproduce." (Animal Societies, Paragraph 2)

(B) "Scientists believe that naked mole-rats developed this cooperative society as the best way to survive." (Animal Societies, Paragraph 5)

(C) "Meerkats also care for young in teams, with both males and females taking turns babysitting the pups." (Animal Societies, Paragraph 10)

(D) "Crows belong to large social groups, sometimes containing thousands of birds." (Crow Families, Paragraph 2)

(E) "This creates tight-knit families in which young crows help their parents care for younger siblings." (Crow Families, Paragraph 2)

(F) "Crows can also be highly selective." (Crow Families, Paragraph 6)

Narrative Writing 1 Answer Key

Item	Answer	CCSS	Score
1A	D	RL.5.4, L.5.4a	/2
1B	A	RL.5.4, L.5.4a	
2A	B	RL.5.1, RL.5.3	/2
2B	D	RL.5.1, RL.5.3	
3	**Winter:** too foreign for comfort **Spring:** like a breath of fresh air	RL.5.1, RL.5.6	/2
4A	A	RL.5.1, RL.5.5	/2
4B	C, E	RL.5.1, RL.5.5	
5A	D	RL.5.1, RL.5.2	/2
5B	B	RL.5.1, RL.5.2	
6	See below	RL.5.1, RL.5.6 W.5.3, W.5.4, W.5.9a L.5.1, L.5.2, L.5.3, L.5.6	/3 [R] /9 [W] /4 [L]
Total Score			**/26**

6 A top response will include a narrative story with the following key points:

- Desiree makes a new friend through a conversation on the phone.
- The story ends in an understandable and positive way that is compatible with the earlier details of the story.

Narrative Writing 2 Answer Key

Item	Answer	CCSS	Score
1A	A	RI.5.4, L.5.4a	/2
1B	C, E	RI.5.4, L.5.4a	
2A	C	RI.5.1, RI.5.7	/2
2B	D	RI.5.1, RI.5.7	
3A	D	RI.5.1, RI.5.8	/2
3B	C	RI.5.1, RI.5.8	
4A	A	RI.5.1, RI.5.2	/2
4B	D	RI.5.1, RI.5.2	
5	"At a dim sum restaurant, servers walk from table to table with rolling carts filled with small, appetizer-like dishes of food."	RI.5.1, RI.5.2	/2
6	See below	RI.5.1, RI.5.2 W.5.3, W.5.4, W.5.9b L.5.1, L.5.2, L.5.3, L.5.6	/3 [R] /9 [W] /4 [L]
Total Score			**/26**

6 A top response will include a description of the following key points:

- Dim sum is a fast-paced meal in which customers choose several small dishes directly off a rolling cart that goes by each table multiple times.
- To get the most out of dim sum, customers should try different dishes and take their time with ordering food.
- The narrative includes techniques that make the description of eating dim sum exciting and even a bit chaotic.

Item	Answer	CCSS	Score
1A	D	RL.5.4, L.5.4a	
1B	A	RL.5.4, L.5.4a	/2
2A	C	RL.5.1, RL.5.2	
2B	D	RL.5.1, RL.5.2	/2
3A	B	RL.5.1, RL.5.3	
3B	Select two of the following: "I am wise beyond my years—wise enough to know that there are issues greater than vending machines." "Vote for me, not because of my age, but because I *will* stimulate change." "I was thrilled to know that the students at McGavin wanted change as much as I did."	RL.5.2, RL.5.3	/2
4A	A	RL.5.4, L.5.4a	
4B	A	RL.5.4, L.5.4a	/2
5A	B	RL.5.1, RL.5.2	
5B	C, D	RL.5.1, RL.5.2	/2
6	Proud Sure Excited	RL.5.1, RL.5.2	/2
7	See below	RL.5.1, RL.5.6 W.5.2, W.5.4 L.5.1, L.5.2, L.5.3, L.5.6	/3 [R] /9 [W] /4 [L]
Total Score			**/28**

7 A top response will include a description of the following key points:

- Both the narrator and the speaker feel doubted because of their age.
- Both try to overcome stereotypes about their age in order to achieve what they believe to be greatness.
- The viewpoints in the passages are meant to provide a lesson for the reader. Age should not necessarily determine a person's ability to lead.

Item	Answer	CCSS	Score
1A	D	RL.5.4, L.5.4a	/2
1B	A, C	RL.5.4, L.5.4a	
2A	C	RL.5.1, RL.5.3	/2
2B	A	RL.5.1, RL.5.3	
3	The completed chart should look like this (rows can be in any order, but the Trait/Evidence pairs must be correct):	RL.5.1, RL.5.3	/2
4A	B	RL.5.4, L.5.4a	/2
4B	C	RL.5.4, L.5.4a	
5A	A	RL.5.1, RL.5.3	/2
5B	D	RL.5.1, RL.5.3	
6	Select these sentences (or a phrase from them): "I forgot we were being timed, but I don't really care if we won or not. Let's just keep building!"	RL.5.1, RL.5.2	/2
7	See below	RL.5.1, RL.5.3 W.5.3, W.5.4 L.5.1, L.5.2, L.5.3, L.5.6	/3 [R] /9 [W] /4 [L]
Total Score			**/28**

Chart for Item 3:

Odin		The Stranger	
Character Trait	Text Evidence	Character Trait	Text Evidence
formal	"'What dost thou want on the Mountain of the Gods?' . . ."	clever	"But the horse did more than this. He set the stones in their places and mortared them together."
giving	". . . he knew that if Asgard were protected, he himself could go amongst men and teach them and help them."	confident	"'. . . I can build great walls that can never be overthrown.'"

7 A top response will include a description of the following key points:

- The events are similar in that characters build a wall within a defined period of time.
- In "The Building of the Wall," the motive to build a wall is safety, and the wall is built with traditional materials that are meant to protect a city from attack. The time span is a year, and the final product is expected to be of high quality.
- In "Up Against a Wall," the motives to build a wall are fun and the challenge of creative competition. The wall is built with nontraditional materials that are meant to pose a challenge to the builders. The time span is twenty minutes, and the final product is expected simply to stand as high as possible; it can be of low quality as long as it stands.

Item	Answer	CCSS	Score
1A	B	RI.5.4, L.5.4a	
1B	D	RI.5.4, L.5.4a	/2
2A	C	RI.5.1, RI.5.2	
2B	E, F	RI.5.1, RI.5.2	/2
3A	Studying species that inhabit alien-like ocean environments could help humans' future survival.	RI.5.1, RL.5.8	
3B	Underline two of the following: • "Other findings could lead to new medical treatments." • "We could also study creatures who survive in strange habitats—without heat, light, or oxygen." • "This could help us discover new ways to survive here on Earth—or among the stars."	RI.5.1, RL.5.8	/2
4	See below	RI.5.1, RI.5.2 W.5.2, W.5.4, W.5.8, W.5.9b L.5.1, L.5.2, L.5.3, L.5.6	/3 [R] /9 [W] /4 [L]
5A	A	RI.5.4, L.5.4a	
5B	C	RI.5.4, L.5.4a	/2
6A	B	RI.5.1, RI.5.3	
6B	A	RI.5.1, RI.5.3	/2
7A	C	RI.5.1, RI.5.3	
7B	D, E	RI.5.1, RI.5.3	/2
8A	A	RI.5.4, L.5.4a	
8B	B	RI.5.4, L.5.4a	/2
9A	D	RI.5.1, RI.5.5	
9B	B	RI.5.1, RI.5.5	/2
10	**"Dive Technology"** • Sylvia Earle holds the record for ocean exploration in a Jim Suit. • Scuba diving equipment limits how deep divers can travel and how long they can stay under water. **Both Passages** • The *Deepsea Challenger* can descend so quickly because of its vertical design. • The *Deepsea Challenger* traveled to the deepest place on Earth. **"Lights, Cameras, Invention!"** • James Cameron has used his films to test out new underwater technology. • Cameron has put some of his movie profits into funding underwater inventions.	RI.5.1, RI.5.6	/2
11	See below	RI.5.1, RI.5.3, RI.5.9 W.5.2, W.5.4, W.5.7, W.5.8, W.5.9b L.5.1, L.5.2, L.5.3, L.5.6	/3 [R] /9 [W] /4 [L]
Total Score			**/50**

4 A top response will summarize the following ideas:

- Earth's oceans, which make up 70 percent of the planet, remain mostly unexplored.
- The oceans contain many different geographical features, many of which are not seen on land.
- The oceans provide different habitats for a wide variety of creatures, most of which are yet to be discovered.
- Exploring the oceans can help us learn more about the planet. Studying creatures living in alien-like habitats could help human survival on Earth and in space.
- The essay will include textual evidence to support all points.

11 A top response might integrate the following ideas:

- Challenging conditions such as darkness, freezing cold, water pressure, and lack of oxygen have made it difficult to explore the oceans.
- Many ocean features, including hydrothermal vents, hot springs, and underwater volcanoes present these dangers, especially in the deepest places.
- Technology like the Aqualung, the Jim Suit, and others are needed to overcome these challenges.
- Ocean explorers who know most about the dangers of diving should help in the invention process. They could help motivate others to find new creative solutions more quickly.
- The essay will include textual evidence to support all points.

Narrative 1 Answer Key				DOK	Difficulty	Score
Item	Answer	Claim #, Target #	CCSS			
1	B	Claim 4, Target 2	RI.5.9 W.5.1a, W.5.1b, W.5.2d, W.5.3a, W.5.3b, W.5.3c, W.5.3d, W.5.3e, W.5.4, W.5.5, W.5.8, W.5.9 L.5.1, L.5.2, L.5.3a, L.5.3b, L.5.6	4	Medium/ High	/1
2	See below	Claim 4, Target 2				/2
3	See below	Claim 4, Target 4				/2
Narrative	See below	Claim 2, Target 2 Claim 2, Target 8 Claim 2, Target 9				/4 [P/O] /4 [D/E] /2 [C]
Total Score						/15

2 Responses should include the following key points:

- The article provides key characteristics that an adventure story should have.
- The two stories are examples of adventures with these same key characteristics.
- Understanding the characteristics of an adventure story can help the reader understand why certain elements are used in the two stories.

3 Responses might include the following key points:

- The bulleted list in the article is most helpful because it provides a summary of the characteristics that are required when writing an adventure story.
- The urgent dialogue in *Swiss Family Robinson* helps to show the tension and excitement related to adventure stories.
- The description in "The Trap" helps to show the action found in all adventure stories.

Narrative A top response includes a multi-paragraph original adventure story that:

- uses details, dialogue, and description to tell a story that has a beginning, middle, and end
- establishes setting, characters, and a plot consistent with characteristics of an adventure as identified in the source article
- relates ideas to tell a logical sequence of events
- expresses ideas clearly using sensory and/or figurative language as appropriate
- has command of conventions, including punctuation, capitalization, usage, grammar, and spelling

[*See* Narrative Performance Task Scoring Rubric]

Narrative 2 Answer Key

Item	Answer	Claim #, Target #	CCSS	DOK	Difficulty	Score
1	See below	Claim 4, Target 2	RI.5.9 W.5.1a, W.5.1b, W.5.2d, W.5.3a, W.5.3b, W.5.3c, W.5.3d, W.5.3e, W.5.4, W.5.5, W.5.8, W.5.9 L.5.1, L.5.2, L.5.3a, L.5.3b, L.5.6	4	Medium/ High	/2
2	A	Claim 4, Target 2				/1
3	See below	Claim 4, Target 4				/2
Narrative	See below	Claim 2, Target 2 Claim 2, Target 8 Claim 2, Target 9				/4 [P/O] /4 [D/E] /2 [C]
Total Score						/15

1 Responses should include the following key points (two from each source):

- The Ancient City of Giza:

  >> Part of the city was dedicated to housing the workers (suggesting that many workers were needed).

  >> Hundreds or even thousands of workers lived in the galleries of the city.

  >> People came from different parts of Egypt to help build it.

- The Great Pyramid: Giza's Ancient Wonder:

  >> It is 480 feet high and made of more than 2 million heavy limestone blocks.

  >> Each block weighed between 2.5 and 15 tons. Some were moved from hundreds of miles away.

  >> It took decades to build.

  >> It required sleds, ramps, and levers to build.

3 Responses might include the following key points:

- "The Ancient City of Giza" is more useful because it tells what life was like for the workers and how they lived when they were not working.

  OR

- "The Great Pyramid: Giza's Ancient Wonder" is more useful because it provides facts about the Great Pyramid, suggesting how the workers built it.

Narrative A top response includes a multi-paragraph narrative that:

- tells about a day in the life of a pyramid worker in ancient Giza
- is written from the point of view of the worker
- uses details and description to tell a story that has a beginning, middle, and end
- establishes setting, characters, and a plot consistent with details identified in the sources
- relates ideas to tell a logical sequence of events
- expresses ideas clearly using sensory and/or figurative language as appropriate
- has command of conventions, including punctuation, capitalization, usage, grammar, and spelling

[*See* Narrative Performance Task Scoring Rubric]

Opinion 1 Answer Key

Item	Answer	Claim #, Target #	CCSS	DOK	Difficulty	Score
1	See below	Claim 4, Target 2	RI.5.3, RI.5.6, RI.5.9 W.5.1a, W.5.1b, W.5.1c, W.5.1d, W.5.2d, W.5.3d, W.5.4, W.5.5, W.5.8, W.5.9 L.5.1, L.5.2, L.5.3a, L.5.3b, L.5.6	4	Medium/ High	/2
2	C	Claim 1, Target 12				/1
3	See below	Claim 4, Target 4				/2
Article	See below	Claim 2, Target 7 Claim 2, Target 8 Claim 2, Target 9				/4 [P/O] /4 [E/E] /2 [C]
Total Score						/15

1 Responses should include the following key points (two of the following):

- Bottled water is convenient. (sources 1, 2, and 3)
- Some people think that bottled water is cleaner than tap water. (sources 2 and 3)
- Some people do not like the taste of tap water. (source 2)

3 Responses should include the following key points:

- The third source would be most helpful because (two of the following):

  » It explains that people incorrectly believe that bottled water is cleaner than tap water.

  » It explains that bottled water companies do not have to follow the same procedures and rules as city water companies.

  » It explains that tap water might actually be cleaner than bottled water.

  » It explains that bottled water might have things in it that are harmful to people.

Article A top response includes a multi-paragraph opinion article that:

- clearly gives an opinion about whether their school should install an improved water purification system and remove all bottled water vending machines
- uses details from the sources to support the opinion
- is well-organized and stays on the topic
- uses clear language to express ideas clearly
- has command of conventions, including punctuation, capitalization, usage, grammar, and spelling

[See Opinion Performance Task Scoring Rubric]

Opinion 2 Answer Key

Item	Answer	Claim #, Target #	CCSS	DOK	Difficulty	Score
1	See below	Claim 4, Target 2	RI.5.9 W.5.1a, W.5.1b, W.5.1c, W.5.1d, W.5.2d, W.5.3d, W.5.4, W.5.5, W.5.8, W.5.9 L.5.1, L.5.2, L.5.3a, L.5.3b, L.5.6	4	Medium/ High	/2
2	See below	Claim 4, Target 4				/2
3	B	Claim 4, Target 3				/1
Article	See below	Claim 2, Target 7 Claim 2, Target 8 Claim 2, Target 9				/4 [P/O] /4 [E/E] /2 [C]
Total Score						**/15**

1 Responses should include the following key points (from two of the following sources):

- Positive aspects of volunteering for community service includes:
  - » Source #1:
    - » Can help others and self
    - » Effort will be appreciated by others
    - » People/animals/environment need help
    - » Very rewarding experience
  - » Source #2:
    - » Helps students better understand the world around them
    - » Helps students see things in new ways
    - » Feel a connection with the community
    - » Can participate with friends
    - » Can learn more about career options
    - » Can inspire students to continue volunteering
  - » Source #3:
    - » Wonderful way to spend time
    - » Can bring many people a lot of joy

2 Responses should include the following key points:

- One of the following pieces of evidence supported by two details from the source:
  - » Helps change students' perspective on life
  - » Helps students learn more about what they like and don't like
  - » Helps students learn more about career options
  - » Provides a basis for a future of community service

Article A top response includes a multi-paragraph opinion article that:

- clearly gives an opinion about whether the school should require students to do community service in order to graduate
- uses details from the sources to support the opinion
- is well-organized and stays on the topic
- uses clear language to express ideas clearly
- has command of conventions, including punctuation, capitalization, usage, grammar, and spelling

[*See* Opinion Performance Task Scoring Rubric]

Item	Answer	Claim #, Target #	CCSS	DOK	Difficulty	Score
1	A	Claim 4, Target 3	RI.5.1, RI.5.9 W.5.1a, W.5.1b, W.5.2a, W.5.2b, W.5.2c, W.5.2d, W.5.2e, W.5.3b, W.5.3d, W.5.4, W.5.5, W.5.8, W.5.9 L.5.1, L.5.2, L.5.3a, L.5.3b, L.5.6	4	Medium	/1
2	See below	Claim 4, Target 2				/2
3	See below	Claim 4, Target 4				/2
Article	See below	Claim 2, Target 4 Claim 2, Target 8 Claim 2, Target 9				/4 [P/O] /4 [E/E] /2 [C]
Total Score						**/15**

2 Responses should include the following key points or similar ideas:

- Source #1:
  - » Objective, unbiased point of view that presents facts and details without opinion
    - » Example – "Laying track was made even more dangerous by the competition between the two companies."

- Source #2:
  - » Mostly objective, slightly biased point of view that presents facts and details but with subjective viewpoint in favor of Chinese
    - » Example – "The men were well organized and met deadlines. Yet, they were still treated unfairly."

- Source #3:
  - » Biased point of view in favor of Charles Crocker
    - » Example – "Impressed with his intelligence and commitment, the company gave Crocker its first construction contract."

3 Responses should include the following key points:

- Students should choose the first source because it describes the state of the nation and the reasons why the Transcontinental Railroad was necessary:
- Details may include:
  - » People had been asking for rail travel across America for decades.
  - » Crossing the country was very difficult at that time.
  - » People were moving out west to mine resources and farm the land. They needed easier access to these resources.

Article A top response includes a multi-paragraph informational article that:

- clearly explains the purpose, challenges, and results of the Transcontinental Railroad
- addresses a specific audience of students and the teacher
- uses details from the sources to support the main idea
- is well-organized and stays on the topic
- uses clear language to express ideas clearly
- has command of conventions, including punctuation, capitalization, usage, grammar, and spelling

[*See* Informational Performance Task Scoring Rubric]

End-of-Year Assessment Answer Key

Item	Answer	CCSS	Score
1A	B	RL.5.4, L.5.4a	
1B	D	RL.5.4, L.5.4a	/2
2A	C	RL.5.1, RL.5.2	
2B	B, F	RL.5.1, RL.5.2	/2
3A	A	RL.5.1, RL.5.6	
3B	B	RL.5.1, RL.5.6	/2
4A	B	RL.5.1, RL.5.5	
4B	C	RL.5.1, RL.5.5	/2
5	Underline two of the following: "For centuries the oak has stood, spreading toward the sky," "Beside it, there's an acorn sending out its first green shoot," "To carry on Earth's steady ebb and flow."	RL.5.1, RL.5.2	/2
6A	B	RI.5.4, L.5.4a	
6B	D	RI.5.4, L.5.4a	/2
7A	A	RI.5.1, RI.5.3	
7B	C	RI.5.1, RI.5.3	/2
8A	D	RI.5.1, RI.5.3	
8B	• She read classified documents. • She wrote notes about information she had gathered.	RI.5.1, RI.5.3	/2
9A	D	RI.5.1, RI.5.2	
9B	B, E	RI.5.1, RI.5.2	/2
10	Paragraph 2, sentence 4 Paragraph 3, sentence 2 Paragraph 4, sentence 3 Paragraph 5, sentence 2	RI.5.1, RI.5.3	/2
11A	A	RL.5.4, L.5.5a	
11B	B	RL.5.4, L.5.5a	/2
12A	C	RL.5.1, RL.5.3	
12B	D	RL.5.1, RL.5.3	/2
13A	C	RL.5.1, RL.5.3	
13B	B	RL.5.1, RL.5.3	/2
14A	A	RL.5.1, RL.5.2	
14B	C	RL.5.1, RL.5.2	/2
15A	C	RL.5.1, RL.5.2	
15B	D	RL.5.1, RL.5.2	/2
16A	B	RL.5.1, RL.5.2	
16B	D	RL.5.1, RL.5.2	/2
17A	He is having bad luck.	RL.5.1, RL.5.2	
17B	Patel himself is responsible for the series of events.	RL.5.1, RL.5.2	/2

Item	Answer	CCSS	Score
18	**The events should be placed in the following order:** 1. Patel decides to put off taking out the trash until the next morning. 2. Patel has to hurry with the garbage and it spills all over him. 3. Because Patel has to change his clothes, he misses the bus. 4. His mom's car won't start, so Patel is late to school. 5. Patel has to stay after school for being late. 6. Patel misses out on playing "Undercover Adventures."	RL.5.1, RL.5.3	/2
19	Five of the following seven words should be in the word web: queen builders workers soldiers caretakers foragers sentries	RI.5.1, RI.5.4	/2
20A	D	RI.5.2	/2
20B	C, F	RI.5.2	
21A	B	RI.5.1, RI.5.3	/2
21B	C	RI.5.1, RI.5.3	
22A	A	RI.5.1, RI.5.2	/2
22B	C, F	RI.5.1, RI.5.2	
23	The following information should be included in the chart in the order noted: **Result:** • tight-knit families • family-specific behaviors **Example:** • young help parents care for siblings • anting	RI.5.1, RI.5.3	/2
24A	D	RI.5.1, RI.5.6	/2
24B	C	RI.5.1, RI.5.5	
25	The following information should be included in the chart: **Type of Animal:** • ant, naked mole-rat • wolf • crow • dolphin • elephant • meerkat	RI.5.1, RI.5.6	/2
26A	B	RI.5.1, RI.5.9	/2
26B	C, E	RI.5.1, RI.5.9	
Total Score			**/52**

PROSE CONSTRUCTED RESPONSE SCORING RUBRIC

Score	READING Comprehension	WRITING Development of Ideas	WRITING Organization	WRITING Clarity	WRITING Language and Conventions
4	[not applicable]	[not applicable]	[not applicable]	[not applicable]	The response shows strong command of standard English conventions with minor errors that do not impact meaning.
3	The response uses text evidence to support an accurate analysis of the text and shows a full understanding of the ideas in the text.	The response addresses the prompt effectively, develops the topic or narrative logically, and is appropriate to the task and audience.	The response is clear and cohesive and has a strong introduction and conclusion.	The response uses language well. It features sensory details, concrete words, transitions, and appropriate vocabulary.	The response shows command of standard English conventions with a few errors that may impact meaning.
2	The response uses text evidence to support a mostly accurate analysis of the text and shows a broad understanding of the ideas in the text.	The response addresses the prompt, develops the topic or narrative, and is mostly appropriate to the task and audience.	The response is mostly clear and cohesive and has an introduction and conclusion.	The response includes concrete words, sensory details, transitions, and/or domain-specific vocabulary.	The response shows inconsistent command of standard English conventions with errors that interfere with meaning.
1	The response analyzes little of the text accurately and shows a limited understanding of the ideas in the text.	The response minimally addresses the prompt, does not develop the topic or narrative logically, and may not be appropriate to the task and audience.	The response is sometimes unclear and lacks a real introduction and conclusion.	The response uses language poorly, with limited details, transitions, and/or domain-specific vocabulary.	The response shows slight command of standard English conventions with numerous errors that interfere with meaning.
0	The response analyzes the text inaccurately or not at all and shows little to no understanding.	The response does not address the prompt.	The response is unclear and incoherent.	The response lacks details, transitions, and/or domain-specific vocabulary.	The response shows little or no command of standard English conventions with consistent errors.

NARRATIVE SCORING RUBRIC

Purpose/Organization

4	3	2	1
Organization fully sustained, clear focus: • an effective, unified plot • effectively establishes setting, develops narrator/characters, and maintains point of view • transitions clarify relationships between and among ideas • logical sequence of events • effective opening and closure for audience and purpose	Organization adequately sustained, focus generally maintained: • evident plot, but loose connections • adequately maintains a setting, develops narrator/characters, and/or maintains point of view • adequate use of transitional strategies • adequate sequence of events • adequate opening and closure for audience and purpose	Organization somewhat sustained, may have an uneven focus: • inconsistent plot, flaws evident • unevenly maintains a setting, develops narrator and/or characters, and/or maintains point of view • uneven use of transitional strategies, little variety • weak or uneven sequence of events • weak opening and closure	Organization may be maintained but may have little or no focus: • little or no discernible plot or may just be a series of events • brief or no attempt to establish a setting, narrator and/or characters, and/or point of view • few or no transitional strategies • little or no organization of an event sequence; extraneous ideas • no opening and/or closure

Development/Elaboration

4	3	2	1
Effective elaboration using details, dialogue, and description: • experiences and events are clearly expressed • effective use of relevant source material • effective use of a variety of narrative techniques • effective use of sensory, concrete, and figurative language	Adequate elaboration using details, dialogue, and description: • experiences and events are adequately expressed • adequate use of source material contributes to the narration • adequate use of a variety of narrative techniques • adequate use of sensory, concrete, and figurative language	Uneven elaboration using partial details, dialogue, and description: • experiences and events are unevenly expressed • weak use of source material that may be vague, abrupt, or imprecise • narrative techniques are uneven and inconsistent • partial or weak use of sensory, concrete, and figurative language	Minimal elaboration using few or no details, dialogue, and/or description: • experiences and events may be vague or confusing • little or no use of source material • minimal or incorrect use of narrative techniques • little or no use of sensory, concrete, and figurative language

Conventions

[not applicable]	2	1	0
	Adequate command of conventions: • adequate use of correct punctuation, capitalization, usage, grammar, and spelling • few errors	Partial command of conventions: • limited use of correct punctuation, capitalization, usage, grammar, and spelling • some patterns of errors	Little or no command of conventions: • infrequent use of correct punctuation, capitalization, usage, grammar, and spelling • systematic patterns of errors

NOTE: For Purpose/Organization and Development/Elaboration, responses that are unintelligible, in a language other than English, off-topic, copied text, or off-purpose should receive a score of **NS** (no score). However, off-purpose responses should receive a numeric score for Conventions.

Copyright © McGraw-Hill Education

Purpose/Organization

4	3	2	1
Clear and effective organizational structure with sustained, consistent, and purposeful focus: • consistent use of a variety of transitions • logical progression of ideas • effective introduction and conclusion • opinion introduced and communicated clearly within the purpose, audience, and task • opposing opinions are clearly addressed (if applicable)	Evident organizational structure with minor flaws; ideas adequately sustained and generally focused: • adequate use of transitions • adequate progression of ideas • adequate introduction and conclusion • opinion is clear and mostly maintained, though loosely • opinion is adequate within the purpose, audience, and task • alternate and opposing opinions are adequately addressed (if applicable)	Inconsistent organizational structure, with evident flaws and somewhat sustained focus: • inconsistent use of transitions • uneven progression of ideas • introduction or conclusion, if present, may be weak • opinion on the issue may be somewhat unclear or unfocused • alternate and opposing opinions may be confusing or not present (if applicable)	Little or no discernible organizational structure, with ideas related to the opinion but little or no focus: • few or no transitions • frequent extraneous ideas are evident; may be formulaic • introduction and/or conclusion may be missing • opinion may be very brief or drift • opinion may be confusing • alternate and opposing opinions may not be present (if applicable)

Evidence/Elaboration

4	3	2	1
Convincing support/evidence for the main idea, effective use of sources, facts, and details; precise language: • comprehensive evidence from sources is integrated • relevant, specific references • effective elaborative techniques • appropriate domain-specific vocabulary for purpose, audience	Adequate support/evidence for the main idea with sources, facts, and details; general language: • some evidence from sources is integrated • general, imprecise references • adequate elaboration • generally appropriate domain-specific vocabulary for audience and purpose	Uneven support/evidence for the main idea, partial use of sources, facts, and details; simple language: • evidence from sources is weakly integrated, vague, or imprecise • vague, unclear references • weak or uneven elaboration • use of domain-specific vocabulary is uneven or somewhat ineffective for the audience and purpose	Minimal support/evidence for the main idea with little or no use of sources, facts, and details; vague: • source material evidence is minimal, incorrect, or irrelevant • references absent or incorrect • minimal, if any, elaboration • use of domain-specific vocabulary is limited or ineffective for the audience and purpose

Conventions

4	2	1	0
[not applicable]	Adequate command of conventions: • adequate use of correct punctuation, capitalization, usage, grammar, and spelling • few errors	Partial command of conventions: • limited use of correct punctuation, capitalization, usage, grammar, and spelling • some patterns of errors	Little or no command of conventions: • infrequent use of correct punctuation, capitalization, usage, grammar, and spelling • systematic patterns of errors

NOTE: For Purpose/Organization and Evidence/Elaboration, responses that are unintelligible, in a language other than English, off-topic, copied text, or off-purpose should receive a score of NS (no score). However, off-purpose responses should receive a numeric score for Conventions.

INFORMATIONAL SCORING RUBRIC

Purpose/Organization

4	3	2	1
Clear organizational structure, purposeful focus: • consistent use of a variety of transitions • logical progression of ideas • main idea stated clearly based on purpose, audience, and task	Evident organizational structure, general focus: • adequate, somewhat varied use of transitions • adequate progression of ideas • adequate statement of main idea based on purpose, audience, and task	Inconsistent organizational structure, somewhat focused: • inconsistent use of transitions and/or little variety • uneven progression of ideas; formulaic • main idea may be unclear and/or somewhat unfocused	Little or no organizational structure or focus: • few or no transitions • frequent extraneous ideas; may be formulaic • may lack introduction and/or conclusion • may be very brief, with confusing or ambiguous focus

Evidence/Elaboration

4	3	2	1
Thorough and convincing support for main idea; effective use of sources, facts, and details: • integrates comprehensive evidence from sources • relevant references • effective use of elaboration • domain-specific vocabulary is clearly appropriate for audience and purpose	Adequate support for main idea; uses sources, facts, and details: • some integration of evidence from sources • references may be general • adequate use of some elaboration • domain-specific vocabulary is generally appropriate for audience and purpose	Uneven, cursory support for main idea; uneven or limited use of sources, facts, and details: • weakly integrated, vague, or imprecise evidence from sources • references are vague or absent • weak or uneven elaboration • domain-specific vocabulary is uneven or somewhat ineffective for audience and purpose	Minimal support for main idea; little or no use of sources, facts, and details: • minimal, absent, incorrect, or irrelevant evidence from sources • references are absent or incorrect • minimal, if any, elaboration • domain-specific vocabulary is limited or ineffective for audience and purpose

Conventions

2	1	0
Adequate command of conventions: • adequate use of correct punctuation, capitalization, usage, grammar, and spelling • few errors	Partial command of conventions: • limited use of correct punctuation, capitalization, usage, grammar, and spelling • some patterns of errors	Little or no command of conventions: • infrequent use of correct punctuation, capitalization, usage, grammar, and spelling • systematic patterns of errors

[not applicable]

NOTE: For Purpose/Organization and Evidence/Elaboration, responses that are unintelligible, in a language other than English, off-topic, copied text, or off-purpose should receive a score of **NS** (no score). However, off-purpose responses should receive a numeric score for Conventions.